Life is Hard

Also by Kieran Setiya

Midlife: A Philosophical Guide

Kieran Setiya

Life is Hard

How Philosophy
Can Help Us
Find Our Way

HUTCHINSON
HEINEMANN

1 3 5 7 9 10 8 6 4 2

Hutchinson Heinemann
20 Vauxhall Bridge Road
London SW1V 2SA

Hutchinson Heinemann is part of the Penguin Random House group of companies
whose addresses can be found at global.penguinrandomhouse.com

Copyright © Kieran Setiya, 2022

Kieran Setiya has asserted his right to be identified as the author of this
Work in accordance with the Copyright, Designs and Patents Act 1988

Book design by Alexis Farabaugh

First published in the US by Riverhead Books in 2022
First published in the UK by Hutchinson Heinemann in 2022

www.penguin.co.uk

A CIP catalogue record for this book is available from the British Library

ISBN 9781529151213

Printed and bound in Great Britain by Clays Ltd, Elcograf S.p.A.

The authorised representative in the EEA is Penguin Random House Ireland,
Morrison Chambers, 32 Nassau Street, Dublin D02 YH68

www.greenpenguin.co.uk

You remind me of someone who is looking through a closed window and cannot explain to himself the strange movements of a passerby. He doesn't know what storm is raging out there or that this person might only with difficulty be keeping himself on his feet.

LUDWIG WITTGENSTEIN

CONTENTS

Preface

This book was conceived before the Covid-19 pandemic. It was written in a fugue of concentration over eighteen months, starting in the summer of 2020, as the world fell apart around me. I'm a philosopher who writes about the question of how to live, and the trials of life had never seemed more urgent. I wanted to acknowledge them.

My relationship with adversity has altered as I've aged. Hardships hit closer to home these days, in my own life and the lives of people I love. Bereavement, cancer, chronic pain: they change the way you see the world. When I was younger, I was more oblivious. I needed the reminder in my epigraph – a remark by the philosopher Ludwig Wittgenstein to his sister Hermine – that people often suffer in ways they don't express. Hardship is routinely hidden.

My relationship with philosophy has changed, too. As a teenager, I loved the abstract theories of metaphysicians, plumbing the basic structure of mind and world. Philosophy was, for me, an escape from ordinary life. I still admire philosophy in its more arcane forms, and I'd defend those forms to anyone. A society that won't support the study of questions about reality and our place in it – even questions science cannot answer – is profoundly impoverished.

But philosophy is, and can be, more than that. To study the discipline is to become an artisan of arguments, learning to dissect and reason through intractable problems. That is what I learned to do in college; it is what I have taught with conviction for many years. Yet I've come to want a philosophy that can speak more intimately to life. When I took my qualifying exams in graduate school, the examiners' report was mostly positive. But I've forgotten all the nice things it contained. What I remember is a critical phrase: my ideas, the examiners warned, had not been 'tested in the crucible of direct moral experience'. My friends and I made fun of that remark. But it stayed with me. The point was less that experience disproved my nascent theories than that those theories were too distant from it.

What would a philosophy look like that was tested in the crucible of direct moral experience? It's an intimidating question. No one's experience is broad or deep enough to stand for everyone's. Our perspective is always limited, with its unique distortions and blind spots. But there could be a philosophy that speaks from one's own life, even as it draws on arguments and thought experiments, philosophical theories and distinctions. It would blur the lines between the argumentative and the personal essay, between the discipline of philosophy and the lived experience of someone who finds philosophy ready-to-hand, a tool with which to work through life's adversities. It would draw us back to the original meaning of 'philosophy' – the love of wisdom – and to philosophy as a way of life.

That's the spirit with which, in troubled times, I wrote this book.

Life is Hard

Introduction

Life, friends, is hard – and we must say so. It's harder for some than it is for others. Into each life some rain must fall, but while the lucky dry themselves beside the fire, others are drenched by storms and floods, both literal and figurative. We live in the wake of a global pandemic and mass unemployment, amid the surging catastrophe of climate change and the revival of fascism. These calamities will disproportionately harm the poor, the vulnerable and the oppressed.

My own luck has been good. I was raised in Hull, an industrial city in the northeast of England that had been through better times. My childhood had its share of troubles, but I fell in love with philosophy, made my way to Cambridge as an undergraduate, moved to the US for graduate school, and stayed. I'm a professor of philosophy at MIT, protected by the wealth and stability of an illustrious if eccentric institution. I have a house, a happy marriage, and a child who is wiser and braver than I ever was. I have never gone hungry or been homeless; I am not a victim of brutality or war. But no one is shielded, in the end, from sickness, loneliness, failure, grief.

Since the age of twenty-seven, I have experienced chronic pain: persistent, fluctuating, strange, a constant drone of sensory distraction. It can be difficult to concentrate and, at times, impossible to sleep. Because it is invisible, my condition is isolating: almost no one knows. (I'll tell you all about it in Chapter 1.) At thirty-five, I had a premature midlife crisis. Life seemed repetitive, empty, just more of the same: a sequence of accomplishments and failures stretching through the future to decline and death. Eight years ago, my mother was diagnosed with early-onset Alzheimer's. Her memory faltered for some time, and then abruptly crashed. I am grieving for someone who is still alive.

As I look around me, I see suffering on a massive scale. When I wrote these words, millions were living in enforced isolation, lonely and desperate due to Covid-19. Many had lost their jobs or could not pay their bills. Loved ones were sick or dying; there was an epidemic of grief. Inequality was rampant and democracy fragile. Another storm is coming, as we fail to heed the fire alarm of global warming.

So what are we to do?

There is no cure for the human condition. But after twenty years teaching and studying moral philosophy, I believe that it can help. This book explains how.

Despite its name, 'moral philosophy' is about much more than moral obligation. As Plato wrote in the *Republic*, circa 375 BCE, 'The argument concerns no ordinary topic but the way we ought to live.' The subject of moral philosophy is expansive, addressed to everything that matters in life. Philosophers ask what is good for us, what ambitions we should nurse, what virtues we should cultivate or admire. They give guidance and they give arguments; they formulate theories by which to live. There's an academic side to this: philosophers study abstract questions and dispute each other's views; they trade in thought experiments that make the familiar strange. But moral philosophy has a practical purpose. Through much of history, there was no clear distinction between philosophical ethics and 'self-help'. It was assumed that philosophical reflection on how to live should make our own lives better.

I accept every part of that. But the aspiration to live well has frequently embraced a more quixotic goal: the best or ideal life. In Plato's *Republic*, justice is imagined through a utopian city-state, not as a fight against injustice here and now. In the *Nicomachean Ethics*, Plato's student Aristotle aims for the highest good, *eudaimonia* – a life that is not merely good enough but one you should choose if you could choose any life at all. Aristotle thought that we should imitate the gods: 'We must not follow those who advise us, being men, to think of human things, and, being mortal, of mortal things, but must, so far as we can, make ourselves immortal, and strain every nerve to live in accordance with the best thing in us.' His answer to the question how to live is a vision of life without deficiency or human need: if you like, it's his version of heaven.

With rare exceptions, even those who set their sights a little lower tend to theorise the good life, not the bad. They focus on pleasure, not pain; love, not loss; achievement, not failure. Not long ago, the philosopher Shelly Kagan coined the term 'ill-being' for 'the elements that directly constitute a life's going badly.' In 'typical discussions of well-being', he observed, 'ill-being is largely neglected'. There's an affinity here with the 'power of positive thinking' that implores us not to dwell on trials and tribulations but to dream of the life we want. Even the ancient Stoics – philosophers explicitly concerned with how to weather life's adversities – were surprisingly upbeat. They believed that we can flourish whatever our circumstance; well-being is entirely up to us. In each of these conceptions, hardship is repressed as we pursue the good.

A premise of this book is that this whole approach is wrong. We should not turn away from hardship; and the best is often out of reach. Striving for it only brings dismay.

This attitude may strike you as perverse or pessimistic. But we need not live our 'best lives' in order to be more resilient; and we have to face the facts. Here's an experience you may have had: you tell a friend about a problem you are coping with, maybe a blowup at work or in a close relationship, a health scare that has you rattled. They are quick to reassure you – 'Don't worry; it will all be fine!' – or to offer you advice. But their response is not consoling. Instead, it feels like disavowal: a refusal to acknowledge what you're going through. What we learn in moments like these is that assurance and advice can operate as denial.

Worse than denial, even, is the urge to justify human suffering. 'Everything happens for a reason' – except, of course, it doesn't. Philosophers have a word, 'theodicy', for an argument that vindicates the ways of God to man. Theodicies address the problem of evil: if God is omnipotent and benevolent, what accounts for the manifold evils of the world? But theodicy has a life of its own, outside of narrowly theistic or doctrinal contexts. Religious or not, we conjure the problem of evil whenever we protest that something should not be; and we engage in something like theodicy when we say it's for the best.

The problem with theodicy is not just intellectual – none of the arguments work – but ethical, too. It's wrong to justify your own or others' suffering, to mute pity or protest in that way. That is the moral of the most famous theodicy of them all. In the Book of Job, the Accusing Angel urges God to test a 'man of perfect integrity', killing his sons and daughters, destroying his property, covering his skin with boils 'from his scalp to the soles of his feet', so that he is left scratching himself with a shard of pottery in the dust. Job's friends insist that he must deserve his fate, a punishment for some cryptic sin. God condemns them 'because [they] have not spoken the truth about me'. Meanwhile, Job protests his innocence. Though the book concludes with what might seem to be redemption – God returns Job's possessions twice over, 'fourteen thousand sheep, six thousand camels, a thousand yoke of oxen, and a thousand donkeys', along with seven brand-new sons and three new daughters – the theodicy falls flat. It's a travesty to think replacements could atone for the loss of Job's first children.

What we should take from the Book of Job is not that virtue is rewarded in the end but that Job's friends were wrong to make excuses for his misery and that it was Job who spoke the truth: we don't deserve to suffer as we do. I'm not saying there is no God, though I don't believe in one myself. I am saying that if God's existence can be squared with the persistence and pervasiveness of hardship in human life, the reconciliation should not temper or negate the fury of compassion, for ourselves and others.

So this is where we are: heirs to a tradition that urges us to focus on the best in life but painfully aware of the ways in which life is hard. To open our eyes is to come face-to-face with suffering – with infirmity, loneliness, grief, failure, injustice, absurdity. We should not blink;

instead, we should look closer. What we need in our affliction is acknowledgement.

That's the impulse behind this book. It's a map with which to navigate rough terrain, a handbook of hardships from personal trauma to the injustice and absurdity of the world. Its chapters make arguments, sometimes finding fault with past philosophers. But the reflection they involve is as much about attending to adversity as it is about arguing around it. As the novelist-philosopher Iris Murdoch wrote: 'I can only choose within the world I can *see*, in the moral sense of "see" [that turns on] moral imagination and moral effort.' It's description more than argument that orients us to life, that tells us how to feel and what to do. It takes work to describe what's really there. Here philosophy is continuous with literature, history, memoir, film. I'll draw on everything I've got.

I said before that moral philosophy and self-help had long been intertwined. This book owes something to that history. Reflecting on the flaws of the human condition can mitigate its harms, helping us to live more meaningful lives. But this is not a self-help book if that suggests 'five tips for overcoming grief' or 'how to succeed without even trying'. It's not the application of an abstract theory, or of the doctrines of some dead philosopher, to the difficulties of life. No magical thinking, no quick fix; instead, the patient work of consolation. To quote the poet Robert Frost, when it comes to human suffering, there's 'no way out but through'.

Two insights light the way. The first is that being happy is not the same as living well. If you want to be happy, dwelling on adversity may or may not be of use. But mere happiness should not be your goal.

Happiness is a mood or feeling, a subjective state; you could be happy while living a lie. Consider Maya, unknowingly submerged in sustaining fluid, electrodes plugged into her brain, being fed each day a stream of consciousness that simulates an ideal life. Maya is happy, but her life does not go well. She doesn't do most of what she thinks she is doing, doesn't know most of what she thinks she knows, and doesn't interact with anyone or anything but the machine. You wouldn't wish it on someone you love: to be imprisoned in a vat, alone forever, duped.

The truth is that we should not aim to be happy but to live as well as we can. As the philosopher Friedrich Nietzsche quipped: 'Humanity does *not* strive for happiness, only the English do' – a swipe at thinkers like Jeremy Bentham and John Stuart Mill, who value nothing but pleasure over pain. I don't mean we should strive to be *un*happy, or be indifferent to happiness, but there is more to life than how it feels. Our task is to face adversity as we should – and here truth is the only means. We have to live in the world as it is, not the world as we wish it would be.

The second guiding light is that, in living well, we cannot extricate justice from self-interest or divide ourselves from others. It will emerge as the book goes on that even the most insular concerns – with one's own suffering, one's loneliness, one's frustrations – are implicitly moral. They are entangled with compassion, with the value of human life, with ideologies of failure and success that obfuscate injustice. Reflecting honestly on affliction in our own lives leads toward concern for others, not into narcissistic self-regard.

Let's not overstate the point. In Plato's *Republic*, Socrates describes a just man stripped of his reputation, falsely accused and prosecuted, 'whipped, stretched on a rack, chained [and] blinded with fire' but doing the right thing all along. For Plato, this man's life goes well. Aristotle sensibly disagrees. It's one thing to act as you should, doing the right thing – Aristotle calls this *eupraxia* – another to live the sort of life you should want to live. Plato's victim achieves the first but not the second. He does what is right; yet we shouldn't want to live like him, in conditions where doing what is right brings terrible costs.

The flaw in Aristotle's view is not that he draws this distinction, which makes perfect sense, but that he concentrates on the life you should want to live, if you could live any life at all – not on the realistic range of good-enough lives. To live well in the sense that animates this book is to cope with the ways in which life is hard while finding enough in one's life worth wanting. Philosophy cannot promise happiness or an ideal life, but it can help to lift the weight of human suffering. We'll begin with the frailties of the body, make our way through love and loss to the structure of society, and end with 'the whole residual cosmos'. Spoiler alert: if you want to know the meaning of life, the answer's in Chapter 6.

The first chapter speaks to something less exalted: the impact of physical disability and pain. I'll explain how the ill effects of disability – and the incremental disabilities of ageing – are commonly misconceived. As activists have argued, but for prejudice and poor accommodations, physical disability needn't make life worse. Their insight is obscured by fantasies of Aristotle's ideal life – a life that is lacking in nothing. But this ideal is incoherent and the activists are right. When we turn from disability to pain, philosophy has limits: it's not an anaesthetic. But it can help us understand why pain is bad, a question much more complex than it seems.

There is solace for those in pain – and a foothold for compassion – in expressing and acknowledging its harms.

Beside physical pain, there's the psychic pain of isolation, loss and failure. Confronting loneliness in Chapter 2, we'll trace the need for society from the problem of solipsism – the view that only the self exists – to the idea that human beings are social animals. We'll find that the harm of loneliness turns on the value of friendship, which turns on the value of other people. In registering this value, love is kindred with compassion and respect. That's why there's relief from loneliness in tending to the needs of others.

The darker side of friendship, and of love, is vulnerability to grief. In Chapter 3, we'll explore the dimensions of loss, from the end of a relationship – I'll write about an ugly break-up – to the end of human life. We'll see how love justifies grief, so that unhappiness is part of living well. The chapter ends with a puzzle that is as much emotional as philosophical. If the fact that a loved one is dead is a reason to grieve, that fact is permanent. It never goes away. Should we then grieve forever? I'll chart the limits of reason in dealing with grief and show how practices of mourning can achieve what reason can't.

Chapter 4 turns to personal failure. Here we'll spend time with furious Buddhists, Prince Myshkin in Dostoevsky's *The Idiot*, and baseball's Ralph Branca. I'll argue that the lure of narrative unity is what makes us 'winners' and 'losers'. We should resist its charms, refusing to narrate our lives in simple, linear ways, or to value project over process. But again, there are limits to reasoning. The shifts in orientation I propose are not ones we can make just by deciding to. We have to work on ourselves, and to fight the ideology that measures human life by what it's able to achieve – a scale that condones grotesque inequities of wealth and social standing.

There is thus a bridge from failure in our own lives to the questions of injustice that preoccupy the last third of the book. In Chapter 5, we'll weigh the critic John Berger's maxim that 'on this earth there is no happiness without a longing for justice'. Drawing on Plato's *Republic*, and on the philosophers Theodor Adorno and Simone Weil, I'll argue that while the unjust may be happy, they do not live well. This isn't the conclusion of some esoteric proof but something we learn by 'reading' the world around us, attending to affliction in our own lives and in others'. The first part of this book thus serves a moral purpose, helping us to work through human suffering on an intimate scale so that we grasp what it means writ large. The chapter ends with our responsibility for justice and the good of taking even one small step towards it.

The final chapters look to the universe as a whole and to the future of humankind. I'll explain how justice could give meaning to human life and how that meaning depends on us. Here existential questions of absurdity collide with climate change: with the urgency of action and the burden of anxiety. We'll end with hope, asking how it earned a place among the ills of life imprisoned in Pandora's box. Confronting my own ambivalence, I'll find a use for hope.

Ultimately, this book is about making the best of a bad lot: the human condition. I offer guidance in adversity, from coping with pain to making new friends, from grieving the lost to failing with grace, from the duties of injustice to the search for meaning in life. There is no simple formula for how to live. What I have instead are stories, images, ideas – some borrowed, some of them my own – and the aspiration to attend, as frankly and humanely as I can, to the problems we face, learning from what I find. Philosophy is not idle speculation or a machine built by argument alone. If you scan the pages to come, you'll find stretches of argument and a lot besides, all of it words that aim to depict the human condition in ways that direct desire. This is not to disparage abstract reasoning, but philosophers have feelings, too.

In the introduction to his book *Morality*, the British philosopher Bernard Williams issued a warning I often recall. 'Writing about moral philosophy should be a hazardous business,' he advised, 'not just for the reasons attendant on writing about any difficult subject, or writing about anything, but for two special reasons. The first is that one is likely to reveal the limitations and inadequacies of one's own perceptions more directly than in, at least, other parts of philosophy. The second is that one could run the risk, if one were taken seriously, of misleading people about matters of importance.' He's right, I think, but the alternatives are worse: impersonality and trivia. Philosophers who address the human condition are bound to disclose themselves in describing the world. I'm afraid that's true of me in writing this book – though when I say that I'm afraid, I mean: I hope.

One

INFIRMITY

You never forget the first time a doctor gives up: when they tell you that they don't know what to do – they have no further tests to run, no treatments to offer – and that you're on your own. It happened to me at the age of twenty-seven, with chronic pain, but it will happen to many of us at some point, with conditions that may be disabling or eventually fatal. The vulnerability of bodies belongs to the human condition.

I don't remember what film we had gone to see, but I know we were at The Oaks, an old arts cinema on the outskirts of Pittsburgh, when pain stabbed me in the side, followed by an urgent need to urinate. After bolting for the bathroom, I felt better, but with a band of tension running through my groin. As the hours went by, the pain resolved into a need to pee, again, which woke me up at one or two a.m. I went to the bathroom – but as if in some bad dream, urinating made no difference. The band of sensation remained, insusceptible to feedback from my body.

I spent a night of hallucinatory sleeplessness sprawled on the bathroom floor, peeing from time to time in a vain attempt to snooze the somatic alarm.

The next day started sensibly, with a trip to my primary care doctor, who guessed that I had a urinary tract infection and prescribed a course of antibiotics. But the test came back negative, as did tests for more abstruse conditions. The pain did not abate. From that point on, the time line is hazy. My memory is poor and medical bureaucracy defeated any attempt to have my records transferred from Pittsburgh to MIT when I moved eleven years later.

But I won't forget the principal episodes. First, a urodynamic study in which I was catheterised, asked to drink a vat of fluids, and made to piss into a machine that measured rate and flow and function. Normal. Second, a cystoscopy in which an apparently teenage urologist projected an old-fashioned cystoscope through my urethra in agonising increments, like a telescopic radio antenna. It certainly felt like something was wrong, but the report again was negative: nothing of clinical interest; no visible lesion or infection in the bladder or along the way. It must have been a busy morning in the clinic, because the doctor and nurse forgot about me after the null result. I gingerly restored my clothes and let myself out, hobbling awkwardly down Forbes Avenue back to the ludicrous Gothic skyscraper in which I worked, the turgid penis of Pitt's Cathedral of Learning looming over me as blood dripped into my underwear from mine.

The final consultation in Pittsburgh was with another urologist. At that point, I was getting used to what I called 'my symptoms' – able to sleep through the discomfort. I was living my life, more or less, with the hum of pain as background noise. The urologist advised me to keep it up. 'I don't know what explains the sensation,' he said. 'There doesn't seem to be a definite cause. Unfortunately, that's not uncommon. Try to ignore it if you can.' He prescribed low-dose Neurontin, an anti-convulsant and nerve pain medication, intended as a sleep aid, and sent me on my way. I'm still not sure if the drug was a placebo. It seemed to help, but I stopped taking it, without discernible effects, a few years later.

And that was that, for roughly thirteen years. No diagnosis; no treatment. I ignored the pain when I could and threw myself into work, nervously enduring flare-ups that would decimate sleep, along with daily life, from time to time. Meanwhile, the rest of my family had their own travails. In 2008, my wife's mother was diagnosed with Stage III ovarian cancer. My mother-in-law is the writer and critic Susan Gubar, who with Sandra Gilbert wrote *The Madwoman in the Attic*, a feminist classic that asked 'Is the pen a metaphorical penis?'. A force of nature, she metabolised her illness through writing, describing with brutal precision the tortuous 'debulking' surgery to remove the most visible tumours, followed by chemotherapy, the painful insertion of drains that failed to relieve a post-operative infection, and her subsequent ileostomy. Her *Memoir of a Debulked Woman* cites writers and artists who have grappled with illness, including a nod to Virginia Woolf, who censured literature's silence on the subject in her essay 'On Being Ill'. Woolf herself was characteristically decorous: 'She may as well not have had bowels, for all the evidence of them in her book,' the novelist Hilary Mantel complained, recounting her own brutal surgery in 'Meeting the Devil'. Susan's book rectifies Woolf's omission, with frank descriptions of struggling to shit after the debulking that removed more than a foot of intestine, her fear of soiling herself in public, the 'bed of pain' to which she was attached for seventeen days as the drains failed to do their job, the excrement that dribbles from the stoma of her 'ostomy', and the persisting disabilities of cancer and its treatment. 'More than half a year after the last chemotherapy,' she wrote, 'my feet were still dead and I could not stand up for more than a few minutes without aches and fatigue setting in.' Despite all this, she has survived so far, against all odds, thanks to a drug trial that worked when a third round of chemo did not.

Meanwhile, her daughter, my wife Marah, was found to have a dermoid cyst on her left ovary – 'dermoid' meaning the kind of cyst that can grow teeth and hair – which had to be surgically removed. She is high risk for breast and ovarian cancer, having inherited the BRCA2 gene from her mother, and is regularly screened. My father-in-law survived open-heart surgery, and back in England, my mother was diagnosed with early-onset Alzheimer's.

I document these trials not because we are unusually stricken – a family of Jobs – but because I'm sure we're not. We all face transient illness and incapacity. And everyone knows someone with cancer, heart disease, chronic pain. In the time of Covid-19, we have friends and relatives who have suffered or died, often in isolation. The fragility of health and everything that depends on it is impossible to ignore. Even the most robust are bound to age, capacities fading as they leave the demographic once dubbed by disability activists 'the temporarily able-bodied'; disability should matter to anyone who is hoping to get old. A non-ideal approach to life does not wish these facts away, leaving the body behind. Instead, it asks how we should live with the malfunctioning bodies we have.

ONE OF THE MOST BASIC LESSONS of recent work in the philosophy of medicine is the need to take care with words. Beginning with the idea of health as the proper functioning of the body and its parts, an emerging consensus contrasts *disease* – a category of malfunction – with *illness*, which is the negative impact of disease on lived experience. Disease is biological; illness is, at least in part, 'phenomenological', a matter of how life feels. It is, as philosophers say, 'contingent' whether or not disease makes life go worse. In general, how well you are able to live when your body malfunctions depends on the effects, which are mediated everywhere by luck and social circumstance. If you have free access to medication, a serious disease like type 1 diabetes may not involve much illness; if you have no health care, a minor infection or dysentery may kill you. The result is that illness is distributed even more inequitably than disease, following lines of wealth, race, and nationality.

Matters are more subtle still with disability, both long-term and the incremental disabilities of ageing. In the last few decades, disability theorists have argued for a social understanding of what it means to be physically disabled. Thus, in *Extraordinary Bodies*, the critic Rosemarie Garland-Thomson aimed 'to move disability away from the realm of medicine into that of political minorities'. It was the work of these minorities that led to the passing of the Americans with Disabilities Act in the US and the

Disability Discrimination Act in the UK. Disability is the focus of a struggle for civil rights.

It has taken time for these ideas to migrate into my corner of philosophy, but a recent book by the philosopher Elizabeth Barnes agrees: 'To be physically disabled is not to have a defective body, but simply to have a minority body.' Garland-Thomson and Barnes do not line up on everything: they differ on the nature or 'metaphysics' of disability. But it is common ground between them – as among many disability theorists and activists – that when you abstract from prejudice and poor accommodations, physical disability does not generally make life worse. Like being gay in a homophobic culture, being disabled may be to one's detriment, but that's a social failing, not a natural inevitability. Physical disability is not, in itself, an obstacle to living well.

It's a claim that provokes both puzzlement and resistance. Philosophers often treat the imposition of disability as a paradigm of injury or harm. And able-bodied people may view the prospect of being deaf or blind or unable to walk with dread. But while it's easy to misinterpret, there is truth in the activists' claim: given adequate accommodations, physical disability need not prevent us from living lives that are, in general, no worse than the lives most people lead.

If physical disability is a category of overt bodily malfunction, it's not akin to illness but disease. Bodily malfunction is biological; its effects on lived experience are contingent, subject to circumstance. That means there is a sense in which physical disability cannot be bad for you in itself. If it makes life worse, that's because it affects how you actually live. A wider moral is drawn in the Daoist parable of the farmer's luck, which I learned from Jon J Muth's radiant picture book *Zen Shorts*. When the farmer's horse runs away, his neighbours sympathise: 'Such bad luck!' 'Maybe,' the farmer replies. His horse returns with two more: 'Such good luck!' 'Maybe,' the farmer replies. The farmer's son tries to ride one of the untamed horses and breaks his leg: 'Such bad luck!' 'Maybe,' the farmer replies. With his broken leg, the son cannot be drafted to fight in a war: 'Such good luck!' 'Maybe,' the farmer replies . . .

So, it all depends. Specifically: whether a physical disability makes your life go better or worse, all told, depends on what effects it has. What is more, a wealth of data attests to the fact that, even in the world as it is, the effects are not so bad: people with physical disabilities do not rate their own well-being significantly lower than other people rate theirs. 'A massive body of research has demonstrated that people who acquire a range of disabilities typically do not experience much or any permanent reduction in the enjoyment of life,' a recent survey of the literature concludes.

For all that, puzzlement persists. There's no denying that needing a wheelchair, or being blind or being deaf, estranges you from things of value: the pleasure of a solitary mountain hike; the look of the scenery; the strains of birdsong in the air. It is in that sense harmful. As the farmer's luck reminds us, there may be collateral benefits. But other things being equal, how can disabilities like these fail to make your life go worse? Isn't that what happens when you take away something good?

The puzzle turns on mistakes about the nature of the good life that go back to Aristotle. It isn't just that Aristotle is preoccupied with the ideal life, the one you ought to choose if everything were up to you, nor that he would regard disability of any kind as incompatible with living well. It is that he thinks the best life is 'lacking in nothing'. It is the 'most desirable of things', to which nothing can be added. If anything good was missing from *eudaimonia*, he argues, adding it would count as an improvement; but it's already the best. This goes along with Aristotle's vision of a single, ideal life, organised around a single activity – contemplation, as it turns out, though the first nine books of the *Nicomachean Ethics* lead us to expect, instead, the life of the accomplished statesman.

Aristotle's monomania is repressed by contemporary authors who recruit him to the project of self-help. Psychologist Jonathan Haidt is typical: 'In saying that well being or happiness (*eudaimonia*) is "an activity of soul in accordance with excellence or virtue",' he writes, 'Aristotle wasn't saying that happiness comes from giving to the poor and suppressing your sexuality. He was saying that a good life is one where you develop your strengths, realize your potential, and become what it is in your nature to become.' But apart from being more sex-positive, Aristotle was saying exactly what Haidt says he wasn't. *Eudaimonia*, for Aristotle, is a life of intellectual excellence, meditating on the cosmos and its laws, or it's a life of practical virtue – of courage, temperance, generosity, justice, friendship, pride – supplied with every gift of fortune. There is no room in Aristotle's thinking for a plurality of good-enough lives, in which individual human beings develop their particular talents, interests and tastes.

The mirage of a life so perfect it is lacking in nothing; the conviction that there is just one path to flourishing: these are ideas we should resist. When I think of my heroes, people who lived good lives if anyone does – none of them perfect – what stands out is how different they are: Martin

Luther King, Jr.; Iris Murdoch; Bill Veeck; a political visionary and activist; a novelist and philosopher; a baseball executive. The list goes on, increasingly scattered: my teacher D. H. Mellor; Talmudic icon Rabbi Hillel; the scientist Marie Curie . . . Feel free to supply a list of your own. I'll bet its members won't have much in common.

What this diversity reflects is a liberalisation of what goes into living well in the long aftermath of Aristotle's ethics. There is not just one activity to love – contemplation or statesmanship – but a vast array of things worth doing, ranging from music, literature, TV, and film to sports, games, and conversation with friends and family from the essential labour of doctors, nurses, teachers, farmers, and sanitary workers to commercial innovation, science pure and applied . . . even philosophy.

It's not that anything goes. Aristotle may have been wrong to focus on a single ideal life, but he was right to affirm that some things are worth wanting, while others are not. Take Bartleby in Herman Melville's incomparable short story, 'Bartleby, the Scrivener'. Narrated by a complacent but well-meaning lawyer who hires the mysterious Bartleby as a copyist, the story pivots on Bartleby's sudden refusal to proofread. Requested to do so, 'Bartleby in a singularly mild, firm voice, replied, "I would prefer not to"'. Things spiral from there. Never giving any reason, Bartleby repeats his mantra. He prefers not to eat anything but ginger nuts; not to talk to colleagues or to check for mail at the post office; not to help the lawyer hold down a piece of tape; not to leave work at all – Bartleby begins to live there; not to answer questions about his life, preferring to be left alone; not to quit the office even when he's fired; not to copy anymore, but also not to move in with the lawyer or to take another job; and when forcibly removed to prison, not to eat – until he dies. We may sympathise with Bartleby, but his desires do not make sense.

Not all preferences are equal, then: there are limits to what is worth wanting. But within those limits, we can flourish in many ways, doing countless different things. Once we absorb this pluralism, the idea that a good life is 'lacking in nothing' begins to seem absurd. It is manifestly false of the lives I gestured at above, all of which have both faults and gaping omissions. It's not as though one should strive to partake in every-thing good, loving every kind of music, literature, art; every sport; every hobby; working as a janitor-nurse-professor-poet-priest.

Karl Marx wrote that in 'communist society . . . it is possible for me to do one thing today and another tomorrow, to hunt in the morning, fish in the afternoon, rear cattle in the evening, criticize after dinner, just as I have a mind'. But even he did not suggest that it was obligatory. When something has value, that doesn't mean we should or must engage with it. At most, it means we should respect it as something worth protecting and preserving. It's fine to be indifferent to free jazz, or classical piano, or death metal: each to their own. But we should want them to survive for others to enjoy. In practice, a good life is selective, limited, fractional. It has good things in it, but the many it must omit don't necessarily make it worse. It's not a blight on my life that I don't enjoy pre-Raphaelite art or know how to build a fence. I have plenty going on.

At the risk of sounding frivolous: this is why physical disabilities don't, as a rule, prevent us from living well. Disabilities prevent us from engaging with valuable things. They are harmful in a way. But no one has access to, or space for, everything of value, anyway; and there's no harm in being estranged from much that's good. Most disabilities leave enough of value in place for lives that are no worse than the majority – and sometimes better.

Bill Veeck started life in baseball as a popcorn vendor for the Chicago Cubs when his father, Bill Veeck, Sr, was club president. He went on to be owner and general manager of a succession of baseball teams: the minor league Milwaukee Brewers, then, in the majors, the Cleveland Indians, St Louis Browns and Chicago White Sox. Veeck worked to integrate baseball, signing the first Black player in the American League. Veeck brought joy to fans even when his teams lost, inventing the now-pervasive shtick that occupies the breaks between innings at baseball games: the music, stunts and audience participation. But he also managed to win, first with the Indians in 1948, then the White Sox in 1959. Veeck installed baseball's first 'exploding scoreboard', which shot off fireworks when the White Sox hit a home run. He did all this while battling an injury suffered in World War II, which led to the amputation of his right foot and eventually much of his leg.

Harriet McBryde Johnson, born with muscular dystrophy, became a lawyer and disability activist. Surviving unexpectedly through middle age, unable to walk, she lost movement in her arms and the ability to swallow most solid foods. Yet Johnson's memoir tells the raucous stories of her protest at the Jerry Lewis Muscular Dystrophy Telethon, an impromptu campaign to sit on the Charleston County Council, a visit to Cuba, being photographed by *The New York Times*, and debating the philosopher Peter Singer, who believes that parents should be able to 'euthanize' infants born with her condition. Her reply to Singer is a pithy expression of my argument. 'Are we "worse off"?' Johnson asks. 'I don't think so. Not in any meaningful sense. There are too many variables.' There is too much diversity, too much contingency, in the prospects for living well.

These are the philosophical foundations of the surveys that indicate how resilient we are: the explanation, and validation, of the finding that people with physical disabilities are, on average, hardly worse off than those without. If it sounds too good to be true, there are two things to say. First, we should ask ourselves why we believe that the lives of those with disabilities are worse than others': do we rely on fear and prejudice, or on meaningful testimony? (Johnson's sensitive account of meeting Singer is itself a means of moral education; everyone should read it.) Second, we should acknowledge complications. For one, there's a distinction between being and becoming disabled. Being disabled is compatible with living a good life, but that doesn't mean that becoming disabled is not traumatic. It often is. What the empirical data suggests, however, is that in most cases, the trauma is substantially more short-lived than we expect.

Sceptical philosophers will ask why it's wrong to impose disabilities on others if they don't make life substantially worse. It's a fair question. Part of the answer is that adapting to disability is hard. Part is that it's wrong to interfere with someone's bodily autonomy, whether or not you do substantial harm. But there's a further point to make. It may be okay to harm someone when doing so prevents a greater harm: you break my leg dragging my unconscious body from the wreckage of a burning vehicle. But it's not okay to cause harm merely when the net result will not be bad. In a mordant thought experiment, the philosopher Seana Shiffrin imagines someone dropping million-dollar bars of gold from a helicopter on to unsuspecting victims, cracking skulls and breaking limbs. The recipients of this largesse may well be glad, on balance, they were hit. They'll recover from the injuries, use the gold to pay their medical bills, and have a wad of cash left over. But what their beneficiary did was wrong. By the same token, causing disability is causing harm – the loss of vision, or hearing, or mobility, say – and it's wrong to do that to someone absent their consent, even if the net result will be a life that is not, on balance, worse.

The final complication is the most significant. I've been generalising about physical disability, talking averages and what tends to happen as a rule. I do not mean for a moment to deny that there are experiences of disability that are profoundly difficult, ones that shatter individual lives. If disability limits your activities too much, if it leaves you with too little of value to do, it may be devastating – and there's no assurance that you will ever adapt. This is where poor accommodations matter most. It's in our collective power to determine how far access to employment, education and social opportunity is affected by physical disability. The problem is a misfit between bodies and the built environment; and the environment can be changed. Schools and employers can be required to accommodate disability and be given the resources they need to do so; buildings can be made accessible. Social policy can minimise the extent to which people with physical disabilities are barred from the plurality of good-enough lives.

Yet even this remains simplistic. We've focused on the aspect of physical disability implicit in its etymology: the lack or loss of an ability through bodily malfunction. To be deprived of access to something good, I've argued, is not by itself to be denied a flourishing life. It's something all of us experience and will endure, increasingly, as we age. But there is another side to many disabilities, and to many forms of illness. Along with the absence of ability, there's the presence of physical pain. The surveys that show that life with a disability is less grim than we might suppose also indicate exceptions. According to a study of older adults led by the economist-philosopher Erik Angner, 'Objective measures [of health] in all but two cases were uncorrelated with happiness . . . debilitating pain and urinary incontinence predict low happiness even when controlling for self-rated health.'

These are the moving parts of almost any infirmity: the deprivation of abilities and the experience of pain. Whether you suffer from cancer, stroke, diabetes or a more transient disease like Covid-19, you can break it down into these elements: lost capacities, bodily suffering – and the anxieties they induce, including fear of death. The same breakdown applies to the effects of ageing. We'll touch on fear of death when we turn to grief and hope. Here we'll treat infirmity by treating its embodiment: first disability, now pain.

I am not physically disabled and to that extent my discussion so far is secondhand: it comes with all the risks and caveats of writing about something you have not experienced. When it comes to the malfunctions of the body, that is happily inevitable: no one has experienced them all. But I have a history with pain and, acknowledging its idiosyncrasies, I can write about its place in an otherwise fortunate life.

———

AFTER THIRTEEN YEARS of relative stability – with occasional flare-ups – things started to go downhill. The pain was burning, tightening, intense enough that I could not mask it with exercise or manage to sleep through it. Now living in Brookline, Massachusetts, I went to see a third urologist. She repeated the basic studies: a urodynamic screening she made me take while standing up, during which I fainted, and another cystoscopy. Although it was much easier than the first, I couldn't bring myself to look at the endoscopic images in real time. She had seen significant inflammation, she said, and proposed a transurethral surgery to correct it.

There were risks, but I was ready to take them – except that I got cold feet. My reservations brought me to urologist number four, who advised that surgery might cause serious complications and offered instead a prescription for antibiotics that I could take when symptoms flared up. It took a few good months for that to happen, at which point I popped the pills, to no apparent effect. Six months further on, during my worst and most relentless phase of pain, including stretches with no sleep at all, I made it to the office of a fifth urologist, whom I still see. I was right to avoid the surgery, he said, but antibiotics wouldn't help. He put a name to my condition – chronic pelvic pain, which means what it sounds like and explains very little – and prescribed an 'alpha blocker'. I'm not sure the medicine helped. But he was the first doctor I'd seen who took my experience seriously, confessed that it was difficult to treat, and talked me through the discouraging prognosis. His acknowledgement was its own small consolation, a step towards writing this book.

There have been many flare-ups since. I finally took medication for sleep – first doxepin, then Ambien, which helped for a few nights but then stopped working – and had another round of screenings. The procedures caused the most sustained and searing pain I have ever experienced, but taught us nothing of use. I went back to living with it, flare-ups ever more frequent, ever harder to ignore.

That pain is bad for you may seem too obvious to warrant scrutiny. But I find myself wondering *why* it is so bad, especially in a case like mine, where the pain I feel from day to day is not debilitating. To my relief, I am able to function pretty well; sleep deprivation is the worst of it. What more is there to say about the harm of being in pain?

Virginia Woolf may have invented the commonplace that language struggles to communicate pain. 'English, which can express the thoughts of Hamlet and the tragedy of Lear,' she wrote, 'has no words for the shiver and the headache.' Woolf's maxim is developed in *The Body in Pain*, a book by the literary and cultural critic Elaine Scarry that has become a classic: 'Physical pain – unlike any other state of consciousness,' she writes, 'has no referential content. It is not *of* or *for* anything. It is precisely because it takes no object that it, more than any other phenomenon, resists objectification in language.'

But as someone who lives with pain, I know that Woolf and Scarry are wrong. Physical pain has 'referential content': it represents a part of the body as damaged or under stress. And we have many words for the quality of pain. As Hilary Mantel protests, replying to Woolf:

> Then what of the whole vocabulary of singing aches, of
> spasms, of strictures and cramps; the gouging pain, the
> drilling pain, the pricking and pinching, the throbbing,
> burning, stinging, smarting, flaying? All good words.
> All old words. No one's pain is so special that the devil's
> dictionary of anguish has not anticipated it.

'Pulsing', 'burning', 'contracting': all good words for mine.

That pain is not a simple sensation but represents the body in distress was argued by the philosopher George Pitcher in 1970: 'To be aware of a pain is to perceive – in particular, to feel, by means of the stimulation of one's pain receptors and nerves – a part of one's body that is in a damaged, bruised, irritated, or pathological state.' Pitcher is on to something, though he makes it sound as though pain is never deceptive. What about the pain an amputee might feel in a body part that they don't have? What about my pain, which doesn't reflect objective damage or duress where the pain appears to be? The fact is that while pain is the appearance of bodily damage or duress, the appearance can be illusory. That doesn't mean the pain isn't real, or doesn't have 'referential content', just that it misrepresents one's body.

This gives rise to a curious reflexivity, the sort of thing philosophers love. Deceptive pain is the most 'meta' of pains. It misrepresents a part of the body as damaged or under stress. That means a system in the body that is meant to track damage or duress – the system of pain receptors – has itself been damaged. It's telling you that something's wrong, when nothing is actually wrong. But that very discrepancy means that something's wrong! So while it mislocates the damage it represents, deceptive pain is never wholly deceptive. You can't be in pain without pathology. Pain doesn't make that mistake.

Whether chronic or acute – the pain of a longstanding syndrome, or pain that is sudden and severe, like a pounding migraine – physical pain represents the body, bringing it into focus. This is how it disrupts our lives. Pain draws attention to itself, taxing our capacity to engage with the world, to enjoy what we are doing, or to disengage entirely through sleep. Whatever activities we've picked from the plurality worth pursuing, pain interferes with our immersion in them. At the limit, when pain is overwhelming, the spotlight of awareness shrinks until there is nothing else. Pain isn't just bad in itself; it impedes one's access to anything good.

When we are healthy, we rarely experience our bodies this way. We 'feel through them', directly aware of the objects and people with whom we interact, barely conscious of the intricate physical means by which we do so. Playing Bach's Organ Sonata no. 4, the organist is not mindful of the countless movements of fingers on keys, but of the music on the page, translated cryptically into notes, melody, rhythm. If she focuses on her fingers, the performance is likely to crash. The paradox is that, as we relax into our bodies, they disappear, becoming a transparent interface – a phenomenon that invites us to think of ourselves as something other than our bodies, an immaterial who-knows-what. Pain draws us back to our corporeality. 'No longer simply a "from" structure,' writes the philosopher and physician Drew Leder in *The Absent Body*, 'the painful body becomes that *to* which [one] attends. As the body surfaces thematically its transitive use is disrupted.'

Even René Descartes, the modern philosopher who championed a 'real distinction' between mind and body – seeing the mind or soul as an immaterial substance – was stopped short by pain:

> Nature . . . teaches me by these sensations of pain, hunger,
> thirst and so on, that I am not merely present in my body as a
> sailor is present in a ship, but that I am very closely joined
> and, as it were, intermingled with it, so that I and the body
> form a unit. If this were not so, I . . . would not feel pain when
> the body was hurt, but would perceive the damage purely by
> the intellect, just as a sailor perceives by sight if anything in
> his ship is broken.

Descartes is floundering here. How can an immaterial soul 'intermingle' with the flesh and blood of a human being? The contrast he wants to draw does not make sense within his dualistic framework of mind and body as wholly distinct existences. Pain shows us that we are not minds somehow tethered to bodies but are essentially embodied. As the French philosopher Maurice Merleau-Ponty writes in *The Primacy of Perception*: 'For us the body is much more than an instrument or a means; it is our expression in the world, the visible form of our intentions.'

What do we gain from philosophical reflection on the body as we struggle to cope with pain? In part, I hope, the solace of being seen and understood. There is a loneliness to pain, an isolation. It is easy to feel like the only one, imagining the pristine lives of passersby. Pain is often invisible. But you are not alone: philosophy bears witness to the suffering that comes with having a body.

There's further solace, of sorts, in the transparency of health, what Leder calls the 'absence' of the healthy body. In the distracting grip of pain, I sometimes feel that I want nothing more than to be pain free. Simply to be at ease, to feel physically well for once, would be the pinnacle of bliss. The feeling is real, but it's one of pain's illusions. For almost as soon as pain is gone, the body recedes into the background, no longer drawing focus, and the anticipated bliss dissolves. The joy of being free from pain is like a picture that vanishes when you try to look at it, or a fabric so soft that it creates no friction and so is nothing to the touch. Attempting to dwell on the absence of pain is like turning on the lights to see the dark.

Philosophers might dub the pleasure of painlessness 'finkish', after a thought experiment in which a live wire is attached to a device that shorts the circuit when the wire is touched; the device is called an 'electro-fink'. Though it carries a current, the wire cannot deliver an electric shock. Closer to home, the French writer Alphonse Daudet, writing in the late nineteenth century while suffering from late-stage syphilis, notes the disappointment of remission: 'The prisoner imagines freedom to be more wonderful than it is. The patient imagines good health to be a source of ineffable pleasure – which it isn't.'

However hard it is to be in pain, however much you want the pain to end, you are likely to exaggerate how good it will feel to be pain free. The projected bliss of painlessness is accessible only to those in pain: it's a finkish experience, one that recedes just as you hope to reach it; you are missing less than you think. This reasoning gives me some relief, if only because I enjoy a paradox. Perhaps it works best for philosophers like me. For others, I concede, the comfort may be cold. Seen from another angle, the elusiveness of absent pain adds insult to injury. Not only does pain feel bad but it gives a false sense of how joyful respite would be. One can look at it both ways: as solace or as slight. Either way, we gain from understanding what pain does, even if what's gained is simply the truth.

PAIN TEACHES THAT we can't escape our bodies or properly appreciate being pain free. But it teaches more than that — about our relation to others and their relation to us. If anything of value has come from my experience with chronic pain, it's a presumptive compassion for everyone else. Concern for one's own suffering is more akin to concern for others than it seems.

Understanding this requires a brief excursion into 'moral theory', the part of philosophy that aims to formulate standards of right and wrong. One of the key ideas of recent moral theory is 'the separateness of persons': ethical trade-offs that make sense within a single life do not make sense when they affect distinct and separate people. If you schedule a root canal treatment, you offset suffering in the near term with relief from later, greater pain: that trade is perfectly rational. By contrast, it's not generally okay to make one person suffer in order to save someone else from harm. The separateness of persons makes the difference.

A similar thought applies when the suffering of many is at stake.

Suppose you had to choose: save one person from an hour of torment or relieve a multitude of mild headaches. Is there a number at which you should save the many, not the one? Consider the pain of the syphilitic Alphonse Daudet. From his fragmentary notebooks:

> Strange aches; great flames of pain furrowing my body,
> cutting it to pieces, lighting it up . . . Crucifixion. That's what
> it was like the other night. The torment of the Cross: violent
> wrenching of the hands, feet, knees; nerves stretched and
> pulled to breaking-point. The coarse rope bound tight round
> the torso, the spear prodding at the ribs. The skin peeling
> from my hot, parched, fever-crusted lips.

Though I joke with my wife about finding Daudet's syphilis relatable, I can barely imagine what his experience was like. If we could relieve his pain or a thousand minor headaches, I am sure we should save Daudet. But what about a million headaches, or a billion, or a trillion?

Philosophers impressed by the separateness of persons deny that the balance tips. The relief of minor pain for many, no matter the number, cannot offset the agony of one, since the pains afflict distinct and separate people. They don't add up. That is why it makes sense to pour money into treatments for rare but agonising illnesses instead of slightly better headache meds. Small gains for many don't outweigh great harms endured by few.

Things seem different when separate people are not involved. The relief of many minor pains for one — for instance, relief of chronic pelvic pain extended over years – *can* compensate for more intense but short-lived pain endured by the very same person. If there was a brutal three-hour surgery, performed without anaesthetic, that would cure my chronic pain, I think I should be willing to go through it. Trade-offs like this make sense within a single life: two thousand weeks of minor pain – the number of weeks I likely have left – cashed in for three hours of agony. But we can't extend this logic to a case with disparate people, ignoring their separateness from one another. If I could save one person from three hours of agony or two thousand from a week of minor pain, it would be wrong to save the many. In this way, self-concern is quite unlike concern for others.

So, at least, I used to believe, before living with chronic pain for eighteen years. I haven't changed my mind about that hypothetical surgery or decided we should sacrifice Daudet. I'd prefer three hours of agony to chronic pelvic pain, but I wouldn't cure a mass of headaches at the cost of Daudet's torment. What I've come to doubt is the analogy between the two. The experience of chronic pain is not like the experience of numerous atomised episodes of pain, differing from the pains of many people only in that they occupy the consciousness of one. The temporality of pain transforms its character.

Although I am not always in notable pain, I'm never aware of pain's onset or relief. By the time I realise it has vanished from the radar of attention, it has been quiet for a while. When the pain is unignorable, it seems like it's been there forever and will never go away. I can't project into a future free of pain: I will never be physically at ease. In *The Absent Body*, Drew Leder, who also suffers from chronic pain, describes its effects on memory and anticipation: 'With chronic suffering a painless past is all but forgotten. While knowing intellectually that we were once not in pain we have lost the bodily memory of how this felt. Similarly, a painless future may be unimaginable.' He is echoing the poet Emily Dickinson, writing circa 1862:

> Pain – has an Element of Blank –
> It cannot recollect
> When it begun – or if there were
> A time when it was not –
>
> It has no Future – but itself –
> Its Infinite contain
> Its Past – enlightened to perceive
> New Periods – of Pain.

One can be trapped by pain: cut off from past and prospect of relief.

It's this confinement I would trade for a brutal surgery. Chronic pain is worse than a mere succession of harms, each distinct and self-contained. What makes it worse is the expectation of pain and the loss of any sense of life without it. This is where the analogy between lasting pain for one and minor pain for many falls apart. It neglects the harms of expectation and memory. If what I was experiencing was just a sequence of atomised pains – with no effect on what I anticipate or recall – I doubt it would make sense to opt for surgery, any more than it makes sense to choose one person's agony over headaches for a million or more. If concern for others would refuse such trades, the same thing goes for self-concern. They are less different than they seem.

There are two lessons here for us. One is that the best approach to any pain of uncertain duration – chronic or acute – is to focus on the present, on what you are doing now, not on what is coming in the future. If you can treat persistent pain as a series of isolated episodes, you can take away some of its power. 'Daudet's advice to his fellow-patients was pragmatic,' writes the novelist Julian Barnes in his edition of Daudet's notes on pain. 'Illness should be treated as an unwanted guest, to whom no special attention is accorded; daily life should continue as normally as possible. "I don't believe I will get better," he said, "and nor does [my doctor] Charcot. Yet I always behave as if my damned pains were going to disappear by tomorrow morning."' I try to emulate Daudet, though I'll admit it isn't easy.

The second lesson is that there is less to the separateness of persons than might appear. If the minor pains of many don't outweigh the agony of one, since they involve distinct and separate people, so a succession of minor pains at distinct and separate times – absent the temporal distortions pain induces – would not be worse than an hour of agony. Such trade-offs falter even when the pains afflict a single subject. A lot has been made of the unshareability of pain, which divides us from one another. In fact, pain is no more shareable across the passage of time. 'Why can one man not piss for another man?' – a question posed by my mother-in-law in a wry rabbinical singsong, shoulders shrugged and palms upturned. But you can't piss, either, for your past or future self.

I'm not denying the loneliness of pain; in a way, I'm amplifying it.

Pain is lonely not just because it separates us from others but because it separates us from ourselves. Still, we can share what we experience, to some degree, by writing or talking about it. And if we can overcome the gulf between past, present and future to sympathise with ourselves at other times – moved by pains that are inaccessible to us now – we can sympathise, too, with the suffering of others. Compassion for ourselves is not the same as compassion for other people, but these sentiments are not as different as they seem. Suffering can be a source of solidarity.

I think this is what the poet Anne Boyer means when she writes about 'un-oneness' in *The Undying*, her book about surviving breast cancer: 'What philosophy often forgets is this: that few of us exist most of the time as just one person. This un-oneness can hurt, just like any oneness can hurt, too.' We can be pained by the pain of others. To remind us of this, Boyer writes, is 'at least one counterpurpose of literature. This is why I tried to write down pain's leaky democracies, the shared vistas of the terribly felt.'

Philosophy needn't forget these facts, about the possibility and pain of compassion for others. It needn't contrast itself with literature or shroud the vistas of the terribly felt. Finding the words to delineate physical suffering, or the experience of disability, is a philosophical task, not something separate from thinking how to feel. It is at once a form of reflection and an act of empathy. I am grateful for Daudet's honesty, which makes me feel less alone. And while exploring one's own suffering can be narcissistic, it needn't be. The most moving passage in Daudet's notebook is not about himself but about the illness of his wife:

Painful hours spent at Julia's bedside . . . Fury at finding
myself such a wreck, and too weak to nurse her. But my
ability to feel sympathy and tenderness for others is still well
alive, as is my capacity for emotional suffering . . . And I'm
glad of that, despite the terrible pains that returned today.

Like Daudet, I am glad that compassion persists in pain, which can help
us to see through our separateness from others, as we see through our
separation from our past and future selves. Yet we must acknowledge that
un-oneness has its limits. Sympathy is difficult to sustain. And beside the
spiritual loneliness of pain – the desire for one's suffering to be seen – there
is the ordinary loneliness of social isolation, which often accompanies it.
As the philosopher Havi Carel writes, the 'natural way in which we engage in social interactions becomes cumbersome in illness, weighed
down by unspoken doubts and discomfort, and the effort required for
genuine communication becomes greater'. It's not inevitable that the ill
should become lonely, though it is more likely; nor is loneliness unique to
them. It's a wider social problem, a hardship we all face to some degree.
What can philosophy learn from loneliness – or teach us about its cure?

Two

LONELINESS

The first poem I remember writing on my own I wrote at the age of seven, waiting for the school day to begin. I had arrived too early and the doors were locked. In a fabricated memory, tumbleweed sweeps across the playground. I open my notebook and inscribe four rhyming lines of verse. 'Out in this so desolate place', the poem begins, figuring the schoolyard as a desert and I a lonesome traveller far from home. Mercifully, I can't recall the rest. What I do recall is a solitary childhood with few friends – though not a very lonely one.

Though I may not have thought much of it then, this distinction matters. The pain of social disconnection, loneliness, is not to be confused with being alone. One can be by oneself, in quiet solitude, without feeling lonely; and one can be lonely in a crowd. There's a distinction, too, between transient or situational loneliness – a reaction to loss or displacement – and chronic loneliness, which persists for months or years. Some are more prone to loneliness than others.

These days, even the least prone may be tested. At the height of the coronavirus pandemic, at the end of March 2020, an estimated 2.5 billion people, one third of the world's population, were in lockdown. Some were quarantined with family, others on their own. The virus was spreading and loneliness was epidemic, too. My own response was a cliché: I started a podcast, *Five Questions*, in which I interview philosophers about themselves. It helped. But I had my wife and child at home, in any case, so little to complain of. Others had it vastly worse: some living utterly alone; some in conditions of abuse; some coping, unaided, with dependents or young children; some in hospital, unvisited, or unable to visit those they loved. The fallout will persist for years.

Even before Covid-19, there was growing concern about the rise of loneliness. In 2018, Tracey Crouch was appointed the first 'Minister of Loneliness' in the UK, publishing a policy document, *A Connected Society*, before resigning, to be replaced by Mims Davies and then Diana Barran. Meanwhile, the US has seen more than seventy years of admonitory books about the subject, from *The Lonely Crowd* in 1950 through *The Pursuit of Loneliness* and *A Nation of Strangers* in the 1970s to *Bowling Alone*, *Alone Together*, and beyond. According to a study that made headlines in 2006 and remains widely cited, Americans were three times more likely to have no one to talk to about 'important matters' in 2004 than they had been less than twenty years earlier, in 1985.

The narrative makes perfect sense: over two centuries, the ideology of 'possessive individualism' – which portrays us as social atoms accumulating private goods – has frayed the fabric of Western society, leaving it threadbare or worse. The word 'loneliness' first appears in English circa

1800. Before then, the closest we get is 'oneliness', which means the state of being alone; like 'solitude', oneliness does not imply emotional pain. Some go so far as to argue that the experience of loneliness, not just the word, originates in 1800. Thus the Romantic poets' reverence for solitary reflection – think Lord Byron in *Childe Harold's Pilgrimage*, Percy Shelley's *Alastor, or The Spirit of Solitude*, William Wordsworth wandering lonely as a cloud in 1804 – gives way to the estrangement of the industrial metropolis captured by Charles Dickens in 1836:

> 'Tis strange with how little notice, good, bad, or indifferent, a man may live and die in London. He awakens no sympathy in the breast of any single person; his existence is a matter of interest to no one save himself; he cannot be said to be forgotten when he dies, for no one remembered him when he was alive.

As a few lonely critics have complained, however, both the data and the history are more complex. Almost as soon as it was published, the 2006 study was challenged by the sociologist Claude Fischer, to substantially less acclaim. His suspicion, that the alleged shift was a 'statistical artifact' – an effect of how the data was collected – was confirmed by subsequent research. It turned out that the 2004 survey altered the order in which questions were asked, affecting the responses; when the questions were flipped back in 2010, the percentage of people with no one to talk to came out lower than in 1985. In his book *Still Connected*, Fischer provides a wealth of evidence that both quality and quantity of social connection have been stable in the US since 1970, although their forms have changed.

As to history: the pain of loneliness was hardly unknown before 1800. If we ask not about the etymology of 'loneliness' but about the desperate need for friends, we find it in Aristotle – 'without friends no one would choose to live' – and, more lyrically, in the work of the Scottish philosopher David Hume, writing in the mid-eighteenth century:

> A perfect solitude is, perhaps, the greatest punishment we can suffer . . . Let all the powers and elements of nature conspire to serve and obey one man: Let the sun rise and set at his command: The sea and rivers roll as he pleases, and the earth furnish spontaneously whatever may be useful or agreeable to him: He will still be miserable, till you give him some one person at least, with whom he may share his happiness, and whose esteem and friendship he may enjoy.

Nor did the Romantic vision of 'that inward eye / Which is the bliss of solitude' die with Wordsworth. It remains alive and well in the poet Rainer Maria Rilke, whose 1929 *Letters to a Young Poet* advised the letters' recipient to 'love your solitude and bear with sweet-sounding lamentation the suffering it causes you'. (In his poem 'New Year Letter', W. H. Auden called Rilke the 'Santa Claus of loneliness'.) More recently, the psychiatrist Anthony Storr praised the generative power of being alone in his 1988 book, *Solitude: A Return to the Self.*

Further complicating the history is that the assumed relationship between loneliness and 'possessive individualism' – the ideology of atomised consumption – gets things back to front. There was indeed a connection between individualism, the rise of the market economy and intimate friendship, but it was the reverse of what is commonly believed. In *The Ends of Life*, Oxford historian Keith Thomas analyses friendship in early modern England, dividing friends into kinsfolk, strategic allies and sources of mutual aid. 'In all these cases,' he writes, 'friends were valued because they were useful. One did not necessarily have to *like* them.' It was the disentanglement of economic and personal life facilitated by the market that made space for private friendships, less subordinate to social need. The great champions of association for pleasure, not utility, were the Scottish Enlightenment thinkers, including Hume's friend Adam Smith, who wrote *The Wealth of Nations*, the bible of industrial capitalism. The market's 'invisible hand' was offered in friendship.

None of this precludes more hostile relations between individualism and intimacy in the course of subsequent centuries. Perhaps we are lonelier now. But a responsible telling of the history of loneliness would acknowledge shifts that trend the other way. Consider, for instance, how little time working-class women, burdened by domestic labour, had available for friendship through the mid-twentieth century, and how much loneliness the stigma attached to being gay has caused. These are both respects in which, relatively speaking, people have more freedom, and are less lonely, now. What is more, the jury is still out on recent developments: it is too soon to say whether social media damage our ability to connect with one another, even as they transform our interactions.

Before the pandemic, then, the evidence for an upsurge of loneliness was inconclusive. Now it's beyond doubt. But even if loneliness were not rampant, it would be a serious problem. Social scientists have quantified the physical effects of being lonely, and the upshots are alarming. Writing with William Patrick, the psychologist John Cacioppo summarised briskly: 'Social isolation has an impact on health comparable to the effect of high blood pressure, lack of exercise, obesity, or smoking . . . chronic *feelings* of isolation can drive a cascade of physiological events that actually accelerates the aging process.' The effects seem to depend on the subjective experience of being lonely, not just 'comorbid' behaviours like poor diet, lack of exercise or excessive use of alcohol. Loneliness triggers a physiological stress response, the inflammation associated with 'fight-or-flight', a cause of decline in physical well-being. In a nine-year study conducted in the 1970s, those with fewer social ties were two to three times more likely to die than those who had more.

From the perspective of public policy, it is important to know these facts. But they point to side effects of being lonely, not the harm of loneliness itself. If you could take a pill that remedied the health impact of social isolation, I suspect that your desire for company would remain. We could look instead at how it *feels* to be isolated. Functional MRIs show that the region of the brain activated by social rejection is the same as that involved in physical pain. But we don't understand why loneliness is bad for us if all we can say is that it hurts. Why does it hurt? And what does that pain tell us about how to live?

WHILE THERE HAVE BEEN lonely philosophers, few have written extensively on the topic. Instead, it shows obliquely in their work. One could tell the history of modern philosophy since Descartes, albeit selectively, as a struggle against solipsism: the idea that nothing but the self exists; we are utterly alone. Meditating in a stove room in 1639, Descartes doubted everything he could – including the existence of other people – in order to rebuild his world on sure foundations. He started with the solitary self: 'I think, therefore I am.' But he went on to prove the existence of God, at least to his own satisfaction. Since God would not deceive us, we can trust our 'clear and distinct perceptions' of the world outside, including other people.

The problem is that Descartes's proof was not convincing. We know we are not alone, but not because we've proved the existence of God. Subsequent philosophers went back to 'I think, therefore I am', contending that Descartes relied on others, even in that solitary stove room. For the German philosopher Georg Wilhelm Friedrich Hegel, writing in the early nineteenth century, we cannot be fully conscious of ourselves except through mutual recognition: there is no 'I' without 'you'. For Jean-Paul Sartre, 'When we say "I think," we each attain ourselves in the presence of the other, and we are just as certain of the other as we are of ourselves.' Then there's Ludwig Wittgenstein, regarded by some as the greatest philosopher of the twentieth century, whose late masterpiece, *Philosophical Investigations*, contends that there can be no 'private language': thought and talk can be moves only in a social practice or 'language game'. Impregnable solitude is impossible.

If these philosophers are right, we have a metaphysical need for one another. Our subjectivity is not self-sustaining: we cannot fully exist, as self-conscious beings, except in relation to other people. It's a profound idea. But it says less about the harm of loneliness than might appear. Since self-awareness has value, a seductive argument runs, whatever it depends on will inherit that value. If we cannot be self-aware except through our relation to others, that relation is valuable in the same way; that is why loneliness is bad. But the inference is flawed. What is necessary for something good need not share its value, any more than the canvas of a beautiful painting, concealed behind the paint, is beautiful, too. In 1923–24, the artist Gwen John made a version of *The Convalescent* that is housed in Cambridge University's Fitzwilliam Museum. Its brittle oils depict a quiet woman in a blue dress seated, reading. I find it very moving. But while the portrait could not exist without its canvas, that doesn't make the stretched cloth moving beneath the paint. The conditions without which something good would be impossible – the canvas of a beautiful painting, the social conditions of self-awareness – need not share the value they sustain.

What makes loneliness bad for us, then, is not that solitude subverts our self-awareness. It's bad for us because we are social animals for whom society is not a given. The harm of loneliness springs from human nature, not the abstract nature of the self.

My solitary childhood wasn't lonely, but it wasn't truly solitary: I was embedded in a family all along. I drew away from them in adolescence – into loneliness. As an inveterate loner, I had little practice making friends. I hadn't learned how to get close to people or how to manage the ups and downs of friendship, how to respond to friction except by withdrawal. A feeling of distance – of being on the margins – settled over me in school and lingered through college. I still find it stressful to interact one-on-one. I am more at ease in conversations sustained by groups, where I feel less pressure to speak. Like many, I have a sense of being left out, excluded from some wider, smoother fabric of social connection, accessible to others. I don't trust that feeling; but I live with it. Human beings struggle with social needs.

Aristotle went beyond this, claiming that 'man is by nature a political animal'. To be political, here, is not just to live in society, perhaps with family or friends, but to belong to a *polis* or city-state. I'm not sure that we are by nature political, in that sense. But we are definitely social. Human beings have always lived together in social groups, from families to tribes and nations. Our distinctive sociality – distinct, that is, from the sociality of great apes and early hominids – rests on the power of joint attention and the 'collective intentionality' through which we conceive ourselves as members of a species. The story of human evolution, in which we developed these capacities, is one of mutual dependence and vulnerability.

That our need for society goes deep is evident in extremes. Infants starved of affection suffer lasting harm. The psychologist John Bowlby was an architect of 'attachment theory' in the 1960s. He was inspired by studies in which rhesus monkey infants preferred a 'surrogate mother' made of huggable cloth to one made of wire, even when the wire surrogate was the source of milk. Comfort mattered more than food. Monkeys deprived of physical contact and isolated from birth would behave erratically when they rejoined the group, alternately fearful and aggressive, rocking back and forth incessantly. Bowlby saw parallel behaviours among homeless children in Europe after World War II. They were seen again among the orphans raised en masse in Romania through the 1980s, under Nicolae Ceaușescu. Bowlby's observations were the impetus for a systematic theory of infant-caregiver 'attachment styles' developed by his student Mary Ainsworth in the 1970s. While the details are debated, no one doubts that early attachment has enduring effects on well-being.

Another extreme is solitary confinement, in which prisoners are kept in 'closed cells for twenty-two to twenty-four hours a day, virtually free of human contact'. At the turn of the nineteenth century, solitary was seen as a path to redemption for criminals in US prisons. But it was no such thing. As Alexis de Tocqueville and Gustave de Beaumont wrote in 1833, convicts were 'submitted to complete isolation; but this absolute solitude, if nothing interrupts it, is beyond the strength of man; it destroys the criminal without intermission and without pity; it does not reform, it kills'. According to a 2014 report by the American Civil Liberties Union, 'The clinical impacts of isolation can be similar to those of physical torture [including] perceptual distortions and hallucinations . . . severe and chronic depression . . . weight loss; heart palpitations; withdrawal; blunting of affect and apathy . . . headaches; problems sleeping . . . dizziness; self-mutilation.' Despite this, solitary confinement is still employed in American prisons, sometimes over periods lasting months or years. It is even used in schools.

The extremes are just that – extremes. But they illustrate the need for human contact that appears in more mundane frustrations: my feeling of disconnection; the apathy and daze of the pandemic, especially for those who live alone; rejection, depression and withdrawal. Loneliness is bad for us because society is central to our human form of life.

This is not to say that having company is always good: the more, the merrier. We have a need for solitude, too. In the late eighteenth century, the philosopher Immanuel Kant wrote aptly of 'the *unsociable sociability* of human beings, i.e. their propensity to enter into society, which, how-ever, is combined with a thoroughgoing resistance that constantly threat-ens to break up this society'. We need others, Kant concedes, but we recoil from being ruled or overwhelmed by them, wanting space of our own. This dual propensity 'lies in human nature'. Kant himself led a notoriously rigid bachelor lifestyle – but was also famous for dinner par-ties rich with conversation.

That we are social animals explains why the desire for company is not like Bartleby's blank preference: we have good reason to spend time with other people. That we vary in our social needs, and that we all need time alone, explains why a plurality of social modes makes sense, some more gregarious than others. For the French poet and novelist Victor Hugo, 'The entirety of hell is contained in one word: *solitude*,' whereas for Sartre – or one of his characters – 'Hell is other people.' At the limit is the hermit or recluse – though it's worth registering that Thomas Mer-ton, a twentieth-century Trappist monk who wrote about the solitary life, believed it 'perilous': 'The essence of the solitary vocation is precisely the anguish of an almost infinite trial.' On the continuum of sociality, most of us fall somewhere in the middle.

We can make sense of loneliness, then, by locating it in human life. We are social animals with social needs; and when those needs are frus-trated, we suffer. 'Loneliness' names our suffering. But we still need to articulate its harms. To appeal to human nature, or to cite frustrated need, is to approach the pain of loneliness from outside. We want to grasp it from within. What makes loneliness so bitter? What makes it so hard?

We could turn to phenomenology, capturing the content of lived experience: to be lonely is to perceive a lack or emptiness, a hole in oneself; the sensation is one of being pushed away, made small or vanishing altogether. But we'll get further if we ask what lonely people miss. The answer is, basically, friends. To understand better what is bad about loneliness – and how it can be remedied – we need to understand why friendship is good.

WE WON'T ALWAYS GO BACK to Aristotle, but in this case we should. For Aristotle is the great theorist of friendship in Western philosophy, devoting two of the ten books of his *Nicomachean Ethics* to *philia*, which is commonly translated as 'friendship'. Along with arguments about the best form of friendship and its place in our lives, Aristotle gives practical tips for coping with unequal friendships – what to do when you love him more than he loves you – and for balancing conflicting obligations, as when you are forced to choose between one friend and another. His wisdom was preserved by Hellenistic thinkers such as Cicero, who wrote a book about friendship in 44 BCE, largely recapitulating Aristotle; and it remains the touchstone for philosophical treatments of what it means to be a friend.

Aristotle's vision of *philia* gets something deeply right. He acknowledges a wide variety of friendships – friendships of utility, of pleasure and of virtue – and he counts familial relationships as forms of friendship, too. We moderns are inclined to make distinctions, both contrasting kin and kindred and distinguishing romantic partners from mere friends, even 'friends with benefits'. Aristotle's more inclusive view is more re-vealing: relationships with family are central to our lives as social ani-mals, fending off loneliness, as romance can also do. When I write about 'friendship' here I mean to include romantic partners and family mem-bers with whom one happens to be close. Frustratingly, we have no word that means exactly this; *'philia'* is too broad, since it includes relation-ships that are purely pragmatic: 'You scratch my back; I'll scratch yours.' Our subject is not mere association, or one's attitude to useful strangers, but the significance of love.

Aristotle's paradigm of friendship is the sort that is based on ethical virtue, a friendship of brave, just, temperate, magnanimous men. Being loved for your character, he argues, is being loved for what makes you *you*; and since love and desire are always for what is good, only those whose character is virtuous can truly be loved for themselves. True friendship, like true virtue, is rare. Archetypes of male bonding in *The Iliad*, Achilles and Patroclus may love each other as true friends; but you and I are probably out of luck.

Thank goodness, it's not so. Friendship may be hard, but not in the way that Aristotle thinks. We can be friends without being heroes or statesmen performing noble deeds. When I picture friends, I think of people having drinks together, laughing at each other's jokes, grieving, sharing stories, watching films, playing games, cooking food. Some of these friends are what I would call 'virtuous' or admirable; others not so much. You may imagine different sorts of people, doing different things. We silently negotiate the terms of our own friendships, adapting and re-vising cultural forms. No doubt there are obstacles to friendship with the vicious: if you would rob me blind the moment you stopped seeing me as a friend, then I'm not sure we're really friends. But notable virtue is not required.

Seeing where Aristotle went astray shows something deep about love for friends and family. His mistake was to think of friendship as meritocratic: for him, it's conditional on virtue. 'But if one accepts another man as good, and he turns out badly and is seen to do so,' Aristotle asks, 'must one still love him? Surely it is impossible, since not everything can be loved, but only what is good.' For Aristotle, friends ought to be flaky, in a way. They should drop you, and stop loving you, the moment you lose the qualities that make you friends. That's pretty much the opposite of the truth. I'm not saying that friendship must be unconditional – but it can be. I've had friendships in which a friend changed utterly, to the point that I no longer liked them. I still cared about them. When my friend becomes an asshole, their redemption matters to me vastly more than that of any random schmuck. I suspect that you're the same.

Aristotle's oversight goes back to his initial argument, that loving someone for himself is loving him for his character. That just isn't so. You are not your character, an assemblage of quirks and traits, virtues and vices, all of which you can outlive. You are a particular, concrete human being, not defined by the attributes you have. Being loved for yourself, therefore, is not being loved for qualities that make you *you*, and being valued as a friend is not the same as being admired. In fact, it's the other way round. Being loved for yourself is being loved precisely *not* for any special qualities by which love must be earned. And to be valued as a friend is to be valued irrespective of your faults.

Philosophers sometimes claim that to love someone is to see the best in them, even to the point of exaggeration; this is known as 'epistemic partiality'. I hesitate to generalise, but that is not my experience. Parents can be unsparingly critical, and whether or not that's for the best, it doesn't conflict with their claim to love. What is more, their children may be happy to reciprocate. Nor is this confined to parental and filial love. No one knows my faults better than my wife, and I know plenty of hers. This doesn't prevent us from loving each other.

All of which helps us locate the value in friendship, and so, by negation, the harm in being lonely. The rewards of friendship are manifold; friendship offers meaning and pleasure of many kinds. But its value flows ultimately, I believe, from the unconditional value of the *people* who are friends. Pick a friendship that matters in your life: it matters, in the end, because your friend matters and so do you. True friends cherish each other, not just the friendship that connects them.

This contrast may seem subtle, but it shows up in the ordinary frictions and resentments of friendship. When I visit you in hospital, there's a difference between doing so for the sake of our friendship and doing so for your sake. I imagine you'd be hurt to learn that I came to visit only to maintain the relationship, or because friendship demands it, not out of direct attachment to *you*. As the philosopher Michael Stocker points out, 'Concern for the friendship is different from concern for the friend.' We tend to focus on the value of the friendship when it needs work – as when we are trying to build it, or the friendship is ailing – or when we are reluctant to meet our obligations to a friend. When things go well, we 'look through' the friendship to the friend herself.

This way of understanding friendship turns on a deeper shift in how to think about the value of human life. It's a defining insight of Enlightenment philosophy that people matter in themselves, regardless of their merits. Kant called this unconditional value 'dignity' as opposed to 'price'. 'What has a price can be replaced with something else, as its *equivalent*,' he wrote, 'whereas, what is elevated above any price, and hence allows of no equivalent, has a dignity.' It is our dignity that love celebrates and loneliness shrouds – a dignity that cries out for respect.

In this way, friendship is entangled with morality. Aristotle was wrong to see true friendship as the mutual appreciation of virtue; instead, it turns on the reciprocal recognition of human dignity. That is why the philosopher David Velleman calls love – the love of romantic partners, family and friends – a 'moral emotion'. This is not to say that a loving friendship is a treaty of joint respect, or that the one implies the other. There can be respect without love; and familiarity may breed contempt. But respect and love acknowledge the same value. As Velleman puts it, respect is a 'required minimum' and love an 'optional' but apt response to the irreplaceable worth of a human being.

True friendship, then, is not a meritocracy. People's talents and virtues may facilitate friendship, as may common pursuits. But friends look through the value of these features to the value of the friend. The friendship matters, ultimately, because the friend does – just like everyone else. This explains what went wrong in that hospital visit, when I came to see you not out of concern for *you* but for our friendship.

And it explains, at last, why loneliness hurts so much. One way to be lonely is to be separated from our friends, and so to miss being with them.

Apart, we cannot reassure them that they matter, and they cannot assure us. Thus the sensation of hollowness, of a hole in oneself that used to be filled and now is not. But there is a more complete form of loneliness, which is to have no friends. When we are friendless, our value goes unrealised. While others may treat us with distant respect, our worth as a human being is unappreciated, unengaged. That's why our reality feels precarious. To be friendless is to feel oneself shrinking, disappearing from the human world. We are made for love; and we are lost without it.

Again, extremes illuminate. Imprisoned for drug offences, most of which were later overturned, Five Mualimm-ak spent more than two thousand days in solitary confinement in the US. Now an advocate against mass incarceration, he wrote about his own experience: 'The very essence of life is human contact, and the affirmation of existence that comes with it. Losing that contact, you lose your sense of identity. You become nothing . . . I became invisible even to myself.' We need the affirmation found in love.

IT'S ONE THING TO DIAGNOSE the harm of loneliness, another to propose a cure. There are no easy answers, in part because loneliness feeds upon itself: isolation kindles fears that exacerbate isolation. But there is a way out, an escape from loneliness predicted by philosophy and confirmed by social science. We'll get to it through fiction, memoir and autobiography.

Haruki Murakami's novel *Colorless Tsukuru Tazaki and His Years of Pilgrimage* begins in the key of Kafka. In his sophomore year of college,

Tsukuru Tazaki endures six months of perfect despair: 'It was as if he were sleepwalking through life, as if he had already died but not yet noticed it.'

> The reason why death had such a hold on Tsukuru Tazaki
> was clear. One day his four closest friends, the friends he'd
> known for a long time, announced that they did not want
> to see him, or talk with him, ever again . . . They gave no
> explanation, not a word, for this harsh pronouncement.
> And Tsukuru didn't dare ask.

When he finds the courage to demand a reason, the only response is: 'Think about it, and you'll figure it out.' But like Kafka's protagonist Josef K., put on trial for inscrutable crimes, Tsukuru has no idea what the reason could be. He is left with neurotic theories that revolve around the names of his four friends, each of which means a colour, where his name means 'create': Tsukuru alone is colourless. Without friends, he drifts through life, dating occasionally, absorbed in his vocation as a railway engineer.

What is most interesting in the novel is the plot twist at its centre: when Tsukuru's casual girlfriend, Sara, urges him to confront his past, the book undergoes a shift in genre. What began as a disorienting parable of our incomprehensibility to one another ends in highbrow soap opera. Tsukuru learns the truth about his friends' betrayal; he is able to accept it; and he admits to himself, and to Sara, that he's in love. As the genres clash, there are notes of paranoia – Sara hints cryptically at 'things I need to take care of', we know not what, then disappears – mixed with bathos and deflating prose: '"There's still something stuck inside you," Sara said. "Something you can't accept. And the natural flow of emotions you should have is obstructed. I just get that feeling about you."'

Murakami's novel tracks the recursive cycle of loneliness – as rejection fractures trust and self-belief – and the radical shift required to make one's escape, like a shift in genre partway through a book. When lonely, one becomes afraid: scared to step outside the stove room of isolation that trapped Descartes, and wary of what one finds whenever one does. In a memoir of chronic loneliness, the author Emily White maps this dynamic: 'I'd tell myself I needed sociability, sociability would present itself, I'd become stressed at the prospect of interacting, and to assuage the sense of stress I'd spend more time alone.' To venture out successfully is to see the world in different terms, not as a place of hazards and sinister secrets, inspired by Kafka, but as a realm of familiar stories, both happy and sad, some of them clichéd, that plot one's relationships with others.

The social science of loneliness attests to its self-reinforcing character. As John Cacioppo argues, the lonely are more attentive to social cues – their threat alert is set to high – but less reliable in interpreting them. They can appear to be less empathic and are less trusting and more negative in their perceptions of others. Lonely people tend to be self-critical, too, attributing social failure to their own faults, not to circumstance – though studies suggest that chronic loneliness does not correlate with any lack of social skills.

It's hard to escape from loneliness without getting help from others, which makes being lonely a catch-22. Nor can one change things overnight: it takes effort to assuage the social anxiety induced by loneliness.

That's why loneliness is a problem for society, not just individuals. As with depression, there is a need to destigmatise loneliness and to fund the mental health care that alleviates it. Towards the end of her book, Emily White describes the work of 'the Dutch psychologist Nan Stevens, who's developed a loneliness-reduction program shown to cut loneliness rates in half'.

> Stevens's program takes the form of weekly group lessons
> offered over the course of three months. Under the guidance
> of a social worker or peer leader, participants are encouraged
> to do straightforward things such as assessing their need for
> and expectations of friendships and mapping out relationships
> that already exist, in order to spot dormant potential
> friendships . . . The program essentially operates as a
> brake on the withdrawal loneliness tends to cue.

But programs like this are frustratingly rare and they are rarely well funded.

In the absence of adequate social services, what are we to do? The guidance offered by psychologists of loneliness fits the picture of love and friendship I've drawn. In Cacioppo's words:

> The most difficult conceptual hurdle for people in the throes
> of loneliness is that, although they are going through
> something that feels like a hole in the center of their being –
> a hunger that needs to be fed – this 'hunger' can never be

satisfied by a focus on 'eating'. What's required is to step
outside the pain of our own situation long enough to 'feed'
others.

The way out of loneliness runs, ironically, through the needs of other people. It's about attending to them, not how they relate to you: concern for a potential friend, not a potential friendship.

What's more, there's continuity between respect and love: between affirming that someone matters, forging a shared compassion, and finally becoming friends. That's why it makes sense, as Cacioppo urges, to 'start small . . . reaching out in simple exchanges at the grocery store or at the library . . . Just saying "Isn't it a beautiful day?" or "I loved that book" can bring a friendly response . . . You sent out a small social signal, and somebody signaled back.' Interactions like these acknowledge the reality of other human beings. This may seem a far cry from the deep connection you crave when you are lonely. But the difference is one of degree or dimension, not kind. Respect, compassion and love are all ways of asserting that someone matters. They are melodies sung in the same key.

It's no accident, then, that Emily White found relief from chronic loneliness in volunteering at a soup kitchen: sympathy and moral outrage can be ways to connect with others. She later joined a women's basketball league. Intimidated by the players, she had paid a non-refundable fee and 'was able to offset [her] anxiety with [her] innate refusal to waste money'. White stuck with it, starting small, with teammates not friends. But she forged a deep relationship with one of them; and in time – not without some setbacks – the two became a couple.

Even when it doesn't end in friendship, paying attention to other people – affirming the value of their lives, not one's own – makes loneliness less harsh. In a 2014 study of commuters in Chicago, participants were asked to engage with strangers on a bus or train, finding out an interesting fact about someone and sharing a fact about themselves; they reported feeling happier afterwards, despite initial misgivings. Or to take an example from my own experience: starting a podcast in the pandemic helped me keep my loneliness at bay. Some of my guests were old friends or teachers; some were acquaintances; some I'd never met. The point was not to build a new relationship but to ask a range of philosophers personal questions about themselves, from the impertinent – 'Do you really believe your philosophical views?' – to the risky – 'What are you afraid of?' The interviews veered from philosophical argument to intimate history, sometimes drawing links between them. One philosopher talked about growing up with strabismus, a condition in which one cannot make eye contact because one's eyes don't properly align. When I asked about childhood loneliness, he traced a path from lifelong social challenges to his work in moral philosophy, which puts reciprocity at the heart of ethics. That conversation was special; but I loved each one in its own particular way. It is astonishing how far someone's individuality, their distinctive way of being in the world, can be disclosed in just twenty-five minutes. After listening intently for half an hour, and editing for an hour more, I would feel less lonely for days.

A podcast may seem artificial. But partly scripted conversation helps to mitigate social anxiety and a growing body of evidence indicates that learning how to listen well is the path to strong relationships. Listening –

really listening – is hard work. As the philosopher Frank Ramsey joked, 'We realize too little how often our [conversations] are of the form: – A.: "I went to Grantchester this afternoon." B.: "No I didn't."' Psychologists and therapists have shown how structured conversation, in which we ask surprising questions and have to pay attention to the answers, helps build intimacy both with strangers and with people we already know.

We tend to think that mutual admiration or common interests must come first in making friends – a distant echo of Aristotle's meritocracy. When we admire someone or share their goals, that makes it easier to become friends. But friendship can begin with the simple act of paying attention. We first acknowledge one another, only later finding things to do. Listening by itself may be enough to forge connection. Doing it well takes courage and resilience. It can be a long, hard path from friendly greetings to close friendship. That path is paved by volunteer work, evening classes, amateur sports. It is paved by invitations offered, silences endured – an exposure of need that may be frightening and touched with shame. To overcome one's loneliness is to open oneself to others when what is opened is a wound.

Even when these strategies work, there are ways of being lonely that they can't address. Seen in one light, the most complete form of loneliness is never having had a single friend. But that condition can be changed. What is irrevocable is the loneliness of loss. New friends cannot replace the dead or permanently estranged. Job was not compensated for the murder of his children by the gift of a second family. If philosophy speaks to love, it must also speak to grief.

Three

GRIEF

In an unflinching stand-up set in August 2012, four days after being diagnosed with breast cancer, the American comedian Tig Notaro spoke about her mother's unexpected death just four months earlier. She described the aftermath to a shaken but still laughing audience at the Largo in Los Angeles:

> My mother just died . . . Should I leave? . . . I can't believe
> you're taking this so hard. You didn't know her. I'm okay . . .
> I was checking my mail and the hospital sent my mother a
> questionnaire to see how her stay at the hospital went . . .
> Hmmm . . . not great . . . did not go great . . . I'll get that
> right to her . . . Question one. During this hospital stay, did
> nurses explain things in a way you could understand? . . .
> considering you had no brain activity.

The emotional confusion of the listener echoes, with refraction, the ringing confusions of grief.

Grief is not a simple emotion. People in grief feel sorrow, yes – but also anger, guilt, fear and moments of lightness as well as depth. The anger may be objectless or the guilt irrational. The fear may be quixotic, directed not at the future but the past. 'I am suffering from *the fear of what has happened*,' wrote the critic Roland Barthes in *Mourning Diary*, six months after his mother died. And then there are those – like Tig Notaro – who joke in the wake of tragedy. Grief is not static, but something that manifests in different feelings at different times. Grieving is something we *do*, if not deliberately – as we perform, deliberately, the rituals of mourning – then in the way we scar when we suffer a bodily wound.

As we will come to see, there are at least three kinds of grief: 'relational grief', which marks a fractured relationship; grief at the harm that befalls someone who dies; and grief at the sheer loss of life. These forms of grief may interact and coincide, but they are not the same. Each of them hurts in different ways and each says something different about love.

Grief's fluidity and polyphony make it challenging to discuss. It's risky to generalise from one's own experience. I was struck by this when I read Joan Didion's celebrated memoir *The Year of Magical Thinking*, which records the bewilderment she felt in the wake of her husband's death. Towards the end of the book, Didion writes, as if for everyone:

> Grief turns out to be a place none of us know until we reach
> it . . . We might expect if the death is sudden to feel shock.
> We do not expect this shock to be obliterative, dislocating to

both body and mind . . . In the version of grief we imagine,
the model will be 'healing'. A certain forward movement
will prevail . . . Nor can we know ahead of the fact (and here
lies the heart of the difference between grief as we imagine it
and grief as it is) the unending absence that follows, the void,
the very opposite of meaning, the relentless succession of
moments during which we will confront the experience of
meaninglessness itself.

The power of this passage partly turns on putting Didion's words in our mouths, but while 'we' are placed in her conception of grief, it may not reflect our own. Speaking for myself: when I think of my wife dying, I find it hard to imagine how life would ever go on. I am expecting the void. (Bad news: my anxiety is predictive. In a longitudinal study of older people, 'those who had earlier revealed this kind of emotional dependency did, in fact, suffer complicated grief reactions'.)

As you can probably tell, I am reluctant to write about grief, predicting or prescribing for others. Unlike loneliness, which I know firsthand, I haven't experienced grief of much intensity myself. For many, that comes first with grandparents. But I did not know mine on my father's side – not even their names, forgetting when or how they died. My maternal grandfather was dead when I was born, and my remaining grandmother suffered from dementia. I barely remember her, and my parents spared me her funeral – a mistake, I think. The closest I have come to grief is watching my mother sail into the darkness of Alzheimer's; but she is still alive.

For insight, I turn to social science. Over the last thirty years, psychologists have made substantial progress in understanding grief. Among their discoveries is that the Freudian notion of 'grief work' as an arduous but necessary grappling with loss is not supported by evidence. The once-conventional wisdom that 'you have to talk about it' risks being wildly counterproductive. In general, studies show, being forced to 'debrief' traumatic events in their immediate aftermath has negative effects on mental and physical health that can last for years, cementing painful memories that one's emotional immune system would otherwise suppress. There is no evidence, either, that grief comes in predictable stages, often graphed in five neat steps: denial, anger, bargaining, depression, acceptance. According to the pioneering grief researcher George A. Bonanno, grief comes not in stages but in waves: 'Bereavement is essentially a stress reaction . . . And like any stress reaction, it is not uniform or static. Relentless grief would be overwhelming. Grief is tolerable, actually, only because it comes and goes in a kind of oscillation.'

It should be no surprise, then, that some of the most faithful documents of grief are fragmentary, non-linear, episodic. Roland Barthes's *Mourning Diary* was scratched out over months on quartered sheets of typing paper. At least as moving, to me, is the French writer Annie Ernaux's diary of her mother's Alzheimer's, written 'hastily, in the turmoil of my emotions, without thinking or trying to marshal my thoughts'. Like grief, the entries are somehow both repetitive and unpredictable.

Perhaps the most interesting attempt to capture grief in prose is by the British experimental novelist B. S. Johnson, who killed himself at forty.

Published in 1969, four years before his death, *The Unfortunates* is a book in a box: twenty-seven booklets to be read in any order, except for 'First' and 'Last'. Its narrator is a journalist assigned to cover a football match in a city he last knew seven years ago, visiting an old friend, Tony, who later died of metastatic cancer. The visit triggers memories that arrive in random order, scattered through the day's events. As chance dictates, he is unable to shake an image, which appears in successive chapters – Tony's mouth, perhaps, 'sallowed and collapsed round the insinuated bones' – or if the order differs, the image returns much later, as a cadence. In the longest chapter, the narrator wrestles a desultory football match into five hundred words of narrative sense. In the shortest two, he is late to Tony's funeral and he learns that Tony has died – the last in a single paragraph that occupies an otherwise blank page. Grief has no narrative order, the book in a box seems to warn; and any closure is temporary. Grief can be opened and reshuffled again and again.

What can we say in the face of grief's complexity, its resistance to narration? According to a long tradition in Western philosophy, the answer is that grief is a pathology, a problem to be solved. But grief is not a mistake; and philosophy should not disown it.

DESPITE THEIR RIVALRY, the warring schools of ancient Greece and Rome – Academic, Epicurean, Sceptical, Stoic – agreed about one thing: grief is no good. Epictetus, a Roman Stoic who was born into slavery, gave brusque directions here:

> With regard to everything that is a source of delight to you,
> or is useful to you, or of which you are fond, remember to
> keep telling yourself what kind of thing it is, starting with the
> most insignificant. If you're fond of a jug, say, 'This is a jug
> that I'm fond of,' and then, if it gets broken, you won't be
> upset. If you kiss your child or your wife, say to yourself that
> it is a human being that you're kissing; and then, if one of
> them should die, you won't be upset.

Good to know! Of course, it's not so easy, not even for Epictetus. But he believed that if we truly knew what it meant that what we love is perishable, if we could inhabit that truth, then we could outsmart grief. 'Alas, my dear friend died.' 'Well, what did you expect? That she would live forever?' So Epictetus asks. But you might expect, or hope, that she would live another year. Isn't that what we want, as a rule, for partners, family, friends? It hurts when death thwarts that desire.

Stoicism was born in ancient Greece in the fourth century BCE; four hundred years later, it was the unofficial ideology of the Roman ruling class. The popularity of Stoic thought, both then and now, depends in large part on its sage advice for managing adversity. This goes beyond defeating grief to a promise of perfect happiness: the secret of self-help. As the Stoics recognised, there are two ways to avoid the frustration of desire. One is to hold your desires fixed and change the world to meet them; the other is to alter your desires to match the world as it's going to be. When the first path isn't open, because you cannot change the world – you want your wife or child to be alive; but they are dead – the second path remains. A fundamental axiom of Stoic philosophy, repeated ad nauseam in the 'Handbook' of Epictetus, is that we should extinguish both aversion and desire for what is out of our control. Focus on what you can change; detach from everything else. If you don't want to be free, claims Epictetus, the fact that you're enslaved won't ruin your life.

If that conclusion makes you nervous, you are not alone. Reviewing a new edition of Epictetus in 1868, the novelist Henry James imagined with alarm how his maxim of serenity under slavery would sound in the pre– Civil War South. For all its appeal, the Stoic axiom is perverse. True: there's no point in attempting the impossible; and we shouldn't blame ourselves for what is out of our control. But to go beyond that, not to care about the things we cannot change, is akin to sour grapes: if I can't have it, then I don't want it. The Stoic attitude may dull our pain, but it does so by distancing us from things that really matter. Think of those who are conditioned to accommodate oppression, as when prisoners and battered wives no longer want the freedom they're denied. It's no good replying, as many Stoics do, that freedom here is a 'preferred indiffer- ent': a thing to be desired, but only with detachment. For it's not irratio- nal to rage against oppression – as at the death of one's wife or child. While grief brings pain, the pain is part of living well: it's inextricable from love.

In fact, there is a gulf between the worldview of ancient Stoicism and that of its recent imitators. For the Greek and Roman Stoics, indifference to what is out of our control draws on a vision of the cosmos as divinely ordered: the world has a mind of its own – for which 'Zeus' is a name – and its agency ensures that what seems bad is for the best. In other words, it rests on a theodicy, not on a platitude about desire. If you believe that Zeus is on your side, I can see why you might be reconciled to what you can't control. If not, adapting what you want to what you can get should seem more petulant than wise. As Virginia Woolf admonished, 'Never pretend that the things you haven't got are not worth having.'

If there is consolation in philosophy, then, it won't derive from killing grief but in knowing how to grieve the way we should. Grief has its reasons: the many forms of loss we mourn, truths that it makes sense to grieve. Even if we focus on lost people – deferring 'climate grief' and grief at the injustice of the world – our grief is multifaceted: we don't just grieve the dead. The goal is to grieve well, not to extinguish grief.

I was introduced to grief myself at age fifteen, when my first girl-friend, Jules, broke up with me. We'd been together for about six months and we had not gone far. Kissing was strictly rationed by Jules 'so that we won't get bored of it'. I think she'd had some bad encounters with boys; I was comparatively tame. But I didn't know how to talk to her and I was prickly and jealous from the start. When Jules got sick of that, she ended things – and I went slightly mad. Though it seems mundane in retro-spect, I found the break-up unintelligible. Why? Why? Why? I called her incessantly, demanding answers. Jules declined to justify herself. She stopped picking up. I kept calling. Eventually, I got over it. The cathartic event was making out with her best friend, whose name I don't remem-ber, at a party I can't otherwise recall. She reported to Jules that I was useless; in my defence, I had limited practice.

The point is that as well as grief around bereavement – which may be what first comes to mind – there is the grief of abandonment. 'You die at heart from a withdrawal of love,' writes the unreliable narrator of Iris Murdoch's novel *The Sea, the Sea*. He is fooling himself, and at fifteen, I did, too. I knew that I would love Jules forever, and that I'd never love again. I was only partly wrong.

We can learn a lot from the comparison between romantic and mortal grief. Romantic grief is about the death of a relationship, not its other half: it's a form of what I called 'relational grief'. When Jules broke up with me, it wasn't for her sake that I grieved, but mine. (She was better off without me.) Other forms of relational grief depend on other relationships, familial or friendly, and have distinctive characters of their own. At the same time, grief can be almost purely non-relational, as when we grieve for those we've never met. In *Baseball Life Advice*, the Canadian author Stacey May Fowles mourns the death of Miami Marlins pitcher José Fernández in a boating accident that took his life at twenty-four: 'There is no real roadmap for dealing with the kind of inexplicable grief that comes with the death of someone we didn't know.' No road map, either, for grief at the death of strangers en masse in a pandemic raging out of our control. Most often grief is both relational (directed at a relationship) and non-relational (directed at the person one loves) – as in the death of a close friend, a partner, parent or child.

These distinctions matter because they refute one of the charges laid at grief's door, sometimes even by the grieving: that it's a form of self-indulgence. Didion's book begins with what might be free verse:

> *Life changes fast.*
> *Life changes in the instant.*

You sit down to dinner and life as you know it ends.
The question of self-pity.

Self-pity is Didion's first thought, after the facts. But while self-pity may be part of grief, we don't grieve only for ourselves: we grieve for the sake of the dead and what they have lost. Grief is not weakness but a token of persisting love.

Even grief that takes in a relationship is not exactly self-centred. If my wife died, I would worry about myself: how will I deal with loneliness or bear the practicalities of parenthood, and daily life, alone? (The question of self-pity.) But I would also grieve for her and for everything she could not be. And I would grieve for *us*, for the loss of what we have together. So much of what I do that matters is what *we* do, impossible without her. Even in my break-up with Jules, what I valued, and lost, was not just someone to make out with or the affirmation that resides in being loved but my relationship with *her*. I may have misread the meaning of that relationship, but it wasn't just about me.

When grief is relational, as it almost always is, grieving well is working through the change that the relationship undergoes. Change, that is, not end. In an essay on the death of friends in older age, the American philosopher Samuel Scheffler introduced a wry vocabulary for relationships that are no longer active. In 'completed' relationships, like my relationship with Jules, the other remains alive; in 'archived' relationships, he or she has died. Even completed relationships are not entirely over: I have a different relation to Jules than I have to perfect strangers. I would say I love her, still, in the way one loves a friend one hasn't seen for years.

Scheffler's point is that archived relationships, also, are not over: they continue to exert a force in our lives. They place demands on us we are compelled to meet, requirements of reverence and respect. We have a relationship with the dead, even if that relationship must change. In almost every account of bereavement I have read, the bereaved has an uncanny sense of the continued presence of the one they have lost. 'This is what those who haven't crossed the tropic of grief often fail to understand,' writes the novelist Julian Barnes in an essay about his wife; 'the fact that someone is dead may mean that they are not alive, but doesn't mean that they do not exist.' In one sense, they do; in another sense, not. 'I talk to her constantly,' he goes on. 'This feels as normal as it is necessary.'

In grieving a relationship, one has to walk the line between a desperate desire that the relationship go on just as it was – that the dead exist just as they did – and a hopeless alienation in which one tries to forget the relationship altogether. It can be difficult to know exactly where one stands. When her son died suddenly, the poet Denise Riley wrote about the temporal dislocations of grief:

> Whenever I need to mention to someone that 'my son died',
> it still sounds to me like a self-dramatizing lie. Tasteless. Or
> it's an act of disloyalty to him. For I don't experience him as in
> the least dead, but simply as 'away'. Even if he'll be away for
> my remaining lifetime.

The risk is that maintaining a relationship with the dead – as it were, long distance – pulls one out of engagement with life. For Riley, time stood still. 'By what means,' she asked, 'are we ever to become re-attached to the world?' And yet the cost of recovery can seem 'intolerably high': 'The dead slip away, as we realize that we have unwillingly left them behind us in their timelessness . . . You would not have wanted this second, now final, loss.'

To grieve well, one must navigate this dilemma: abandon the dead and be disloyal, or cling to them as they were and suffer. The way through, however hard, is to accept that one's relationship must change without conceding that it's over. In a memorable rant, the philosopher Palle Yourgrau castigates authors who dedicate their books to the memory of the dead: 'It's your mother who taught you to love music, not your memories of your mother, your father who first took you to a poetry reading, not your memories of your father . . . What could be more different from a *dead* parent than a *living* memory?' We should dedicate books to the dead themselves, not to our recollection of them. A fact of metaphysics – the dead are not unreal; we can still speak of them, have relationships with them – easily misplaced in the fog of grief.

I have no guide for how to alter one's relationship with the dead – or, for that matter, with the living, when they leave. Each relationship is particular, its own world, and generalities are out of place. Nor is anything I've said intended as a cure. My point is that there need not be disloyalty or betrayal in accepting change. One can do things to memorialise the dead, alone or in the company of others, but one cannot do things *with* them. That's not abandonment, any more than one abandons one's child when one does less for them as they grow up, or betrays one's parents in taking care of them where they once cared for you. But it sometimes feels that way.

Reflecting on the death of his wife, C. S. Lewis called bereavement a 'universal and integral part of our experience of love. It follows marriage as normally as marriage follows courtship or as autumn follows summer. It is not a truncation of the process but one of its phases; not the interruption of the dance, but the next figure.' It's more difficult to assume this attitude towards the death of a child than it is with partners and friends – one does not expect to see one's children die. But to find a way through grief is to sustain a relationship on new terms. That costs us pain, but it is not only painful. Those who recover well from grief find pleasure and comfort in memories of the loved dead. Lewis wrote: 'The more joy there can be in the marriage between dead and living, the better . . . The better in every way. For, as I have discovered, passionate grief does not link us with the dead but cuts us off from them.' That the dead cannot be happy is hard to bear; to think of them without happiness is worse.

WE GOT HERE BY DRAWING a distinction. There is grief at the fracture in a relationship; and there is grief for the sake of the dead, what Barthes called 'Pure mourning, which has nothing to do with a change of life, with solitude, etc. The mark, the void of love's relation.' Dealing with the first grief leaves the second grief untouched. But here, again, the ancient schools agree: death does no harm to the one who dies and so it makes no sense to grieve for *them*.

It would be nice to think that death is harmless and therefore nothing to fear. But the arguments for this conclusion are unfortunately weak. The hedonist Epicurus, a self-help guru who set up a compound for disciples in Athens called 'the Garden' in 306/7 BCE, argued that death cannot harm us because we cease to be conscious when we die and thus do not feel pain. 'So death, the most terrifying of ills, is nothing to us,' he continues, 'since so long as we exist, death is not with us; but when death comes, then we do not exist. It does not then concern either the living or the dead, since for the former it is not, and the latter are no more.' But this is sophistry. While non-existence saves you from certain evils – pain, in particular – you don't need to exist in order to miss out on life. The harm of death is the harm of deprivation, of pleasures forfeited, relationships unravelled, projects incomplete. When one is dead, one's activities are circumscribed. (This is true even if one continues to exist in some spiritual form: one does not get to carry on one's mortal life.) We are harmed by death in that it would be better to live on, if we could live well. Grief may register this harm: 'Look what *she* has lost, now that she has lost life,' writes Barnes on the death of his wife. 'Her body, her spirit; her radiant curiosity about life.'

The harms of deprivation are real: it's bad not to get what would be good. But it's not as simple as that. For we do not grieve when we're deprived of good things that no human being gets. In my book *Midlife*, I wrote about a friend who wanted to be Superman, faster than a speeding bullet, more powerful than a locomotive, able to leap tall buildings in a single bound. Who wouldn't want that? But I imagined him in pain, agonised by his merely human powers, as we are agonised, at times, by the prospect of death. His response seems disproportionate, irrational: it makes no sense to weep at the absence of capacities that go beyond the human frame. Does it make sense, then, to weep at our mortality, which belongs to the human condition? Why grieve for someone who has lived their four score years and ten, any more than we grieve our inability to fly?

When a loved one dies young, what they miss is not a superhuman life but an ordinary one. We should feel grief at that. It's different when they die at ninety, peacefully, after living well enough. That is no misfortune: it's about as good as it gets. We may be sad that they missed out on more, but we shouldn't grieve that fact the way we grieve an early death. Grief when a grandparent dies is not the same as grief when a child does. And yet we grieve. For what? What is the object of our grief, if not the deprivation of a good-enough life? It is the bare fact of oblivion.

Just as grief divides into grief for one's relationship and grief for the sake of the dead, so grief for the dead divides into grief at the harm of dying – the years they should have had – and grief at the sheer loss of life. All three forms of grief are expressions of love: to value a relationship; to want what is good for the one you love; and to cherish their existence. Love, like grief, is complicated.

I can feel its filaments begin to fray as my mother fades. I recall the summer in the Cotswolds when she started to repeat what others said as if it had occurred to her unbidden. 'England's green and pleasant land,' my wife had mused, as the countryside flowed by the passenger window of the car. A minute later, my mother in the backseat: 'This reminds me of that poem, you know – "Jerusalem" – our green and pleasant land.' I'd always found the poem sinister. She was diagnosed with Alzheimer's some twelve months later, seemed stable enough for several years, then began to slip last Christmas. It's hard to tell how she is doing now when I talk to her on the phone. She still remembers me, comments on the weather and on going for a walk. She remembers where she is, and that her memory is failing – but she does not know what the day has held or what it will, and she can't sustain a conversation. Her life has contracted, diminished. My father, once a doctor, is her full-time caregiver. I want her to live; but there may come a time.

I've been reading Annie Ernaux's *I Remain in Darkness*, a book named for the last words her mother wrote, suffering from Alzheimer's, before she was moved to the hospital in which she died. Ernaux writes unsparingly in what were private notes, published without revision a decade later. The month her mother is hospitalised: 'This morning she got up and, in a timid voice: "I wet the bed, I couldn't help it." The same words I would use when I was a child.' Ten months later, her mother begins to know she won't recover. 'It breaks my heart,' Ernaux writes. 'She is alive, she still has desires, plans for the future. All she wants is to live. I too need her to be alive.' Another year or so, less than a month before she died:

> I hand her an almond bun; she can't eat it on her own, her lips
> suck wildly at thin air. Right now, I would like her to be dead
> and free of such degradation. Her body stiffens, she strains to
> stand up and a foul stench fills the atmosphere. She has just

relieved herself like a newborn baby after being fed. Such horror and helplessness.

Even wanting her mother dead, saved from indignity and suffering, Ernaux is 'overcome with grief' when her mother dies. 'That's it. Yes, time has stopped. One just can't imagine the pain.'

Not easy words for me to read, but I want to know what the future holds. For Ernaux, love fragments: she wants the best for her mother, to be 'free of such degradation' and so to die; and yet she grieves her death, not just, I think, for the relationship wrecked but for the value of her mother's life – the dignity affirmed by love, which recoils from death. We found this value at the root of friendship. It is also at the root of grief at the sheer loss of life.

There is a kind of comfort in this bleakness, that we are never wrong to grieve. Even where there is no relationship to reshape, no special misfortune to mourn, love registers a fact that tells us how to feel: the fact that a particular human being is no more. Unhappiness is part of living well, of facing the truth and responding as we should. If we did not grieve, we would not love.

THESE FACTS GIVE RISE to a puzzle that is as much emotional as philosophical. If the fact that a loved one is dead is a reason to grieve, that fact is permanent. It never goes away. Should we then grieve forever?

Thankfully, most of us don't. According to empirical research on grief, more than half of those who lose a partner or child are 'emotionally resilient', rebounding after two or three months; others adapt in a year or eighteen months; only a small proportion experience prolonged or chronic grief. They may need exposure therapy or cognitive behavioural intervention.

In one way, the news is good: 'Most bereaved people get better on their own, without any kind of professional help,' the psychologist George Bonanno writes. 'They may be deeply saddened, they may feel adrift for some time, but their life eventually finds its way again, often more easily than they thought possible.' In another way, it's disturbing. Does our resilience mean that we no longer value the life of the one we've lost or that we never really did? Two months after his mother died, Roland Barthes asked himself: 'Does being able to live without someone you loved mean you loved her less than you thought . . . ?' The philosopher Berislav Marušić echoes Barthes in a moving essay on grief:

> I was surprised that only a few weeks after my mother's death,
> I could lead my life more or less exactly as I did before her
> death: I hardly missed a beat! . . . The grief seemed to
> disappear almost completely . . . In grieving, it seemed to me
> that my grief would continue for as long as her death was a
> reason to grieve – that is, as long as she continued to matter
> to me . . . When we anticipate the diminution of grief, it
> seems to us that, in time, we will no longer care about
> our loss.

We may not want to grieve forever; but we don't want this. We don't want to stop loving the dead, to stop caring about them, to stop registering their loss for what it is. If the reason for grief is that someone we love is dead, and they stay dead, why should we cease to grieve? That they've been dead for years, or that we've grieved for months: these facts don't diminish their loss. The non-existence of the dead remains as absolute as ever. How can we make peace with the fact that grief subsides?

Like other emotions, grief is a response to reasons: facts that seem to justify the feeling. Anger balks at insult or injury; fear registers potential threats; and grief represents loss. Perplexity at grief's subsidence turns on the premise that reasons alone dictate what we should feel: that how it makes sense to grieve is settled by the facts to which our grief responds. If that were true, we should never cease to grieve for those who die. But that isn't how grief works. As time passes, grief alters not because the reasons for it change – we don't react to news about the duration of our own grief, as if to say, 'Now a year has passed, it doesn't matter so much that she's dead' – but because grieving is something we do, in time, as part of human life. It's not an emotional state but an emotional process, one whose shape is not fixed by the reasons to which it responds.

Grief is not unique. The same thing goes for love. Love grows and deepens over time: what was fondness can become the bond of decades. Though it isn't bound to happen, and it isn't always a good thing when it does, this development makes perfect sense. But why? Is the fact that we've loved someone another year another reason for love, as though putting in the time makes them more lovable? No. It's not that, in loving someone, we attend to facts about the history of love, tracking its duration in our lives and so adjusting our affections. (Our focus is directed outwards, at those we love, not at our own experience.) It is that love, like grief, is an emotional process, not a state. Love's evolution is a part of what it is.

This means there is a way in which the waning of grief, and the increase of love, will always seem unintelligible from within. They can be understood as phases in the course of human emotion, but they don't respond to changes in the object of love, or grief. The dead stay dead and neither time nor tears will make that better, even if they make it easier to bear. It is, I think, the elusiveness of reasons for diminished grief that makes the rituals of mourning so essential. The practices by which we process grief, in private and in public, fill the rift that reasons leave.

One of the first funerals I attended was in my first year teaching at the University of Pittsburgh. Rob Clifton, a beloved philosopher of physics, died of colon cancer at the age of thirty-eight. I remember vividly two things about his funeral, a Christian service at the Church of the Ascension in Oakland, close to Pitt's secular Cathedral of Learning. The first was a note Rob left to be read aloud, expressing impish delight at having forced his atheist colleagues to attend a religious ceremony. The second was the community that visibly encircled his grieving wife and kids: the Sunday school class, the families joined by something more than simple friendship. As research attests, resilience in grief correlates with social support, as well as personal and financial flexibility. But there was more to it than that. What I envied was the air of knowing what to do when someone dies, knowing how to structure days that might otherwise be directionless.

Each culture makes its map of the terrain through which we stumble, uncertainly, in grief. There is the Jewish tradition of sitting shiva, mourning in the company of friends for seven days. The Dahomey of Western Africa celebrate the life of the deceased with drinking, dancing, singing and dirty jokes. The Saramaka in Surinam hold communal 'rites of separation' that culminate in the exchange of fantastic folk tales, allegories of the human condition. In China, the legacy of polytheism survives in rites that emulate the burial of kings beside their servants and possessions with the use of paper replicas; practice matters more than belief. In the West, the regulation of grief goes back at least to classical antiquity. The historian David Konstan quotes a funerary law from ancient Rome on which 'parents and children over six years of age can be mourned for a year, children under six for a month. A husband can be mourned for ten months, close blood relations for eight months. Whoever acts contrary to these restrictions is placed in public disgrace.'

Konstan speculates that Aristotle – who is exceptional among ancient philosophers in not condemning grief – omits it from his theory of emotion in the *Rhetoric* because, unlike anger or fear, it has no natural resolution. In anger, one avenges or accepts insult or injury; in fear, one flees or faces a potential threat. And then it's over. Grief isn't like that, at least when it's about the loss of life. There's nothing you can do to extinguish the reasons for grief short of bringing the loved one back to life. That's why we need practices of mourning and the direction they provide. Map in hand, we navigate what reason can't.

For much of Western history, not just grief but death itself was ritualised. There were conventions for dying at home with family, friends and neighbours. Children were included in the rites, which were at once routine and profoundly serious. Death became more private through the nineteenth century. According to the anthropologist Geoffrey Gorer, a further shift took place in World War I, when the rituals of mourning were defeated by the numbers of the dead. By the late twentieth century, death outside the home – in a hospital or hospice – had become the norm; dying is a process overseen by doctors and nurses. I am not here to pass judgement on these changes, only to state a problem that many confront, which is the relative absence of meaningful social practices through which to experience grief. We are given only skeletal structures of mourning and have to construct the body for ourselves.

There's something similar in love. As the conventions of the marriage plot lose authority, fewer people feel the need to marry at all; those who do are free to make up rituals of their own. I don't disparage it – I did it myself – but I do think something's lost: the off-the-shelf intelligibility that tradition brings. When my wife and I got married, we had difficulty finding an officiant. The first person we asked turned out to be an evangelical radio talk-show host. (Long story.) He did not want to participate in a 'pagan' ceremony. The parting was mostly amicable and entirely mutual. Cautioned, we began to search for someone with both gravity and flexibility. We found Bob Epps, a retired campus minister at Indiana University. (The wedding would take place at my mother-in-law's house in Bloomington.) Our meeting with Bob was reassuring. A placid barrel of a man, he had seen everything. Leaning over the table towards us, he made a pyramid of his hands and stated his few provisos: he was happy to do whatever we liked, but no livestock or drugs *during* the ceremony. We were willing to go along with that. At last, we reached the sticking point: it wouldn't feel like a wedding to me, I told him, unless we used the Book of Common Prayer – but I didn't want 'God' to be there. 'Whether you mention him or not,' Bob smiled benignly, 'God is going to be there.' That felt right.

When I think about mourning my mother or, God forbid, my wife or child, what I want is the equivalent of this: as much of the tradition I recognise as I am able to accept. Grief is not naturally narrative. It comes in a chaos of waves and fluctuations, undetermined by reason. No wonder we find comfort in the dubious theory of stages. But what we need is not a theory; it's a practice. Conventions of mourning give a structure to grief it would not otherwise have. They make the possibility of grieving well more legible.

While I was writing this book, in January 2021, my father-in-law died suddenly of an apparent heart attack. Edward Gubar was laid-back, loyal, smart and intellectually omnivorous, a sometime writer and journalist who taught in the Honors College at Indiana University. He loved his students, poker and progressive politics, and he had turned his gambling itch into a fruitful sideline in cryptocurrency. We hadn't seen him since the pandemic started and his death still seems unreal. The weeks after he died were a scramble of activity for my wife, Marah; her sister, Simone; and Edward's partner, Christine, everything complicated by Covid-19. Only Christine could be there in person, managing a welter of logistics.

Mourning was disrupted by distance. We sat shiva over Zoom, but disembodiment makes it hard to measure the loss of a concrete human being – and impossible to share the comfort of a hug. Meanwhile, the planning of the Zoom memorial, tracking down lost friends and family members, seemed to put Marah's grief on hold. The event itself was something to cherish, despite the occasional audio glitch: a communion of far-flung friends and family that would not have taken place in ordinary times, eliciting stories about Edward from kindergarten and high school, his time as a taxi driver in New York and as the coach of Marah's softball team, his boundless gift for hanging out, lingering endlessly after meals in restaurants or chatting on the phone. Some told funny anecdotes; others wept: grief's polyphony played out. When we looked at the recording afterwards, we saw that a handful of friends had stayed on, sharing memories, when we had gone: hanging out in honour of Edward.

It was only after the memorial that Marah really cried, grieving in ebbs and flows. She is visited by the ghosts of Sunday phone calls that she will not make. But it is hard for her to feel that Edward is really gone, when he was virtual for months. Her grief is in suspended animation. It is harder for others. The pandemic disrupted not just mourning but the rituals of death itself. Patients were forced to die alone, watched by their loved ones on computer screens. There is a great mass of suspended grief. Even before Covid-19, for many, the rituals of mourning were fragile or vague in ways that limit their efficacy: we're not sure what to do when someone dies.

To mourn when rituals are absent or disrupted is to improvise. One has to lean much harder on the logic of relational grief, shifting one's relationship with the dead in ways that honour their existence. Deprived of familiar rites when Edward died, we were forced to invent our own. We watched women's college basketball – the Indiana Hoosiers in the NCAA Tournament – for the first time in years, and talked about Edward's love of college sports. On what would have been his birthday, we bought a lottery ticket in his memory, and lost. More lastingly, Marah vowed to keep in closer touch with distant friends, inspired by Edward's gift for friendship. In one of her crystalline microfictions, the writer Lydia Davis asked 'How Shall I Mourn Them?' and answered with more questions: 'Shall I keep a tidy house, like L.? . . . Shall I hold many grudges, like B.? . . . Shall I wear only black and white, like M.?' It is up to those who grieve to ask such questions for themselves, finding ways to mourn that echo the lives of the lost. These personal modes of mourning bear more weight when impersonal modes are out of reach.

Nor is tradition or practice an antidote to grief. Our situation may be harder without ritual, but it is never easy. Even as it heals, the scar of loss may open again. Grief has no permanent solution: there is perpetual ambivalence. 'For here is the final tormenting, unanswerable question,' writes Julian Barnes: 'What is "success" in mourning? Does it lie in remembering or in forgetting? A staying still or a moving on? . . . The ability to hold the lost love powerfully in mind, remembering without distorting?' Sometimes a question is unanswerable not because it's hard to know the answer but because the question presupposes something false. The premise, here, is that we can succeed or fail in grief once and for all. But the desire for narrative closure is at odds with grieving well. While the conventions of mourning lend structure to grief, it's not the structure of beginning, middle and end. It's an atlas for the hardest stretch of grief that leads into uncharted but habitable terrain. If life is a story, grief reminds us, then it does not have a happy ending. Perhaps it's not a story, after all.

Four

FAILURE

Failure is a many-splendoured thing. We fail at work, in love, in our obligations to one another. But there is a special dignity to those who fail in sports. Nowhere is failure more well defined, more irrefutable. Sports are often pressed upon the young as a place in which to learn how to cope with failure, how to handle it with grace. And yet they are home to the most incurably catastrophic moments of inadequacy and error.

Consider baseball, a sport that is both philosophically resonant and linguistically well served. Here we find 'Merkle's Boner': in 1908, Fred Merkle of the New York Giants fails to touch second base and is tagged out by Johnny Evers on what would have been a winning hit in a decisive game. There's the 'Snodgrass Muff': Fred Snodgrass drops an easy catch, costing the Giants the World Series in 1912. And there's Bill Buckner, struck by 'the Curse of the Bambino', the near century of frustration allegedly caused by the sale of Babe Ruth's contract by the Boston Red

Sox in 1918. Sixty-eight years later, an easy ground ball trickles through Buckner's legs and the Red Sox lose the championship to the New York Mets. Perhaps the greatest failure of them all is Ralph Branca, who gives up the 'Shot Heard 'Round the World': the Bobby Thomson home run that wins a crucial play-off game for the New York Giants, sending them – and not the Brooklyn Dodgers – to the 1951 World Series.

How does one live with conclusive failure? It's a question for everyone, even if it cuts sharper and deeper for some. Projects worthy but frustrated or forgotten are endemic in life. 'If we remembered even a fraction of our million tiny plans,' writes the poet-aphorist James Richardson, 'our whole lives would be regret at their failure.' There is comfort to be found in the sheer pervasiveness of projects gone awry. In a self-described 'book of solace', the British social critic Joe Moran regales us with narratives of failure great and small, culminating with an artist 'who neither learnt from his failures nor wished to learn', who completed few paintings, and whose most famous fresco began to flake before he died, the result of a failed experiment. The artist was Leonardo da Vinci.

Failure is typically more mundane. When their plans fall flat, my kid likes nothing better than to hear about the wreckage of mine: romantic fiascos, flunked tests, athletic defeats. A particular favourite: my failure to make it out of the DMV car park the first two times I took my driving test, when their mother was nine months' pregnant with them. I was able to drive her to hospital to give birth only because she was in the car with me, meeting the terms of my learner's permit. I passed my driving test the third time around, in the company of my bemused but supportive father-in-law. He distracted me from nervousness with failures of his own, as when his car got stuck in reverse and he had to drive his date home backwards.

Not much is at stake in failures like these. In others, the world turns upside down – or fails to. One of the great studies of social failure is *The Experience of Defeat*, by the British historian Christopher Hill. The execution of King Charles I in 1649, at the height of the English Civil War, opened prospects for social democracy that were previously unthinkable. The Levellers pushed for the redistribution of wealth and the extension of rights to the poor. The more trenchant Diggers, led by Gerrard Winstanley, embraced communism two centuries before Marx. Winstanley proclaimed Earth 'the common treasury of all' and ignited an experiment in practical utopianism, cultivating the wasteland of St George's Hill, Surrey, and nearby Cobham Heath, without claim to ownership, on behalf of anyone in need. Winstanley hoped that others would follow suit, that landowners would lose their serfs and be forced to join his ad hoc community, that private property would simply fade away. That is not what happened. The Diggers were crushed by local landowners, who sued them in the courts and burned the houses they had built on the commons. A radical vision of the future failed with them.

Failure is so prodigious, so multiform, so widespread that it's impossible to survey comprehensively. In that sense, this chapter is bound to fail. It focuses on personal failure – the failure to achieve ends or goals that are important to you – setting moral and social failure aside. (They will resurface as we go on.) It is in personal failure that you risk defining your life, becoming a loser. This definition takes place, refined and purified, in great moments of failure in sports.

What is it like to be synonymous with failure? And what does that tell us about the ordinary failures of our lives? Having given up the Shot Heard 'Round the World, Ralph Branca suffered his fate with little protest for fifty years. Anyone who knew anything about him knew that he threw the fastball Thomson hit; many knew nothing more. In *The Echoing Green*, the journalist Joshua Prager unwinds the knot that binds Branca and Thomson together. What he tells is not a story of redemption, of failure expunged; it is too late for that. Instead we learn what we knew all along: how much more there was to Branca's life, and to Thomson's, than the moment that connects them. Prager interrupts the season right before the play-off to narrate in synchrony their prior lives: Branca's huge and happy family, Thomson's supportive brother and taciturn father. The intermission takes up a fifth of the book. The final game itself is paused as Thomson steps into the batter's box before the pitch – the swing – Russ Hodges's call: 'The Giants win the pennant! The Giants win the pennant!' – to begin the day: 'Pitcher and hitter had both awakened that morning at 7:30 in the home of parents,' Prager writes. 'Both had eaten eggs prepared by his mother, Thomson with a side of bacon, Branca a side of ham.'

No one's life can be reduced to one event, one enterprise or one ambition. Each is made of facts and facts and facts. Nor is there any fate to be discerned in what transpires. As we relive the season, the moment, we see how differently things could go, the sheer contingency of failure and success. More than that, we see how tempting and how dangerous it is to tell the stories of our lives as if they had some hidden teleology, driving onwards to predestined ends. Prager fights the inertia of retrospection that sees each episode as what was going to happen all along. He contests it in the structure of his book – doubling back on his protagonists' lives in detours that suspend the sequence of events – and in the structure of his sentences, which explode or invert expected syntaxes, as if to step outside of time. From the first few pages:

> Thus did a bloody digit and enflamed appendix now convene Durocher [the Giants' manager] and Horace Stoneham [their owner] in New York's center-field clubhouse . . . Durocher was obnoxious, would from short instruct his pitcher to throw at opposing batters . . . All about [Brooklyn] were starting nines, and the consequence most embraced of its newfound proficiency was the overtaking of New York.

There are dozens more like this throughout the book: verbs, prepositions, subordinate clauses, scattered through sentences to surprise the reader. You never know how it will all turn out.

Prager's play with form puts failure in perspective. 'The foundational myth of failure is that it's our own fault,' writes Joe Moran. We can be at fault for failure, but the chaos of contingency in life – the pitch that dips or doesn't, the catch that bounces from the heel of a glove – reminds us that control is never absolute and often limited. Whatever your mistakes, moreover, there is more to you than the failures they explain, more than any project you pursue. The tendency to miss this, or obscure it, turns on how we narrate our lives, pared down to pivotal moments, and on the kinds of narrative we are encouraged to give. The experience of failure and the stories we tell about ourselves are as closely entwined with each other as the lives of Branca and Thomson. To loosen the hold of failure, we need to ask how far life is, or is not, narrative.

THE IDEA THAT WE NARRATE our lives to ourselves, and that doing so is part of living well, is sufficiently commonplace that its most vocal critic, the philosopher Galen Strawson, could describe it as 'a fallacy of our age'. He lists an impressive roster of advocates, including the neurologist and author Oliver Sacks ('Each of us constructs and lives a "narrative" . . . this narrative *is* us'), the psychologist Jerome Bruner ('We *become* the autobiographical narratives by which we "tell about" our lives') and a murderers' row of philosophical big hitters: Alasdair MacIntyre, Daniel Dennett, Charles Taylor and Paul Ricoeur. For Taylor, a 'basic condition of making sense of ourselves [is] that we grasp our lives in a *narrative* . . . as an unfolding story'. And for Dennett, 'We are all virtuoso novelists, who find ourselves engaged in all sorts of behaviour, more or less unified . . . and we always try to put the best "faces" on it we can. We try to make all of our material cohere into a single good story. And that story is our autobiography.'

It sounds appealing, in a way. Who doesn't think they have a brilliant memoir in them? But the question isn't rhetorical: many of us don't think that and a lot of the rest are kidding themselves. 'I have absolutely no sense of my life as a narrative with form, or indeed as a narrative without form,' Strawson writes. And yet he seems to be living quite well.

Strawson's biography is a useful case study. His father was P. F. Strawson, the Waynflete Professor of Metaphysical Philosophy at Oxford, one of the most eminent philosophers of the late twentieth century. Strawson senior is known for his humane defence of freedom and responsibility and for a conception of ourselves as fundamentally embodied beings. His son Galen was precocious, gripped from the age of four by puzzles of infinity and death. After a detour through Islamic Studies at Cambridge, Strawson junior went to Oxford to read philosophy, becoming a well-known author and professor. What is he famous for? A strident attack on the possibility of freedom and responsibility and an insistence that we introspect ourselves as something distinct from the human beings that bear our names.

The irony is perfect: Galen Strawson, arch critic of Life as Narrative, lives one of the oldest stories in the book – a philosopher's rendition of 'killing the father'. We can use this irony to separate three elements in Life as Narrative and to extricate ourselves, a little, from the grip of failure. The first element is the conjecture, nicely verbed by Strawson, that we are bound to 'story' ourselves, presenting our lives as coherent narrative wholes. The other elements are ethical: that a good life must form a coherent narrative, and that it must be one whose subject tells that narrative to himself. Strawson's own example pulls the last two elements apart. His life can be told as a story, more or less, but I know from correspondence with him that the story isn't one that Strawson tells. If we trust his testimony, he does not story himself at all. Strawson is an exception to the psychological conjecture that we are bound to tell our lives in story form. If his life is good, he shows that the subject of a good life need not tell its story – even if there is a story to be told.

Now, one example is just that. But there are plenty more. Like me, you may be one of them, living from day to day and year to year without much sense of narrative direction. Strawson cites illustrious forebears, among them Iris Murdoch and the mercurial pioneer of the personal essay, Michel de Montaigne. To these we might add Bill Veeck, who served in the army, managed baseball clubs to failure and success, and fought to integrate the American League. All three had lives that were dense with things worth doing, some done exceptionally well, along with miscues, misdirections, swerves. That's enough for a good life, without the need for a story that ties it all together. To see one's life as a narrative arc, heading for a climax that it may or may not reach, is to see it as a potential failure; but one need not live that way.

Consider Murdoch, who studied classics, worked in the civil service in World War II, became a philosopher for ten years, then quit to be a full-time novelist. Throughout, she was pansexual and polyamorous, despite her long marriage to John Bayley, an English professor at Oxford. There were plenty of hurt feelings. Murdoch went on to write twenty-six novels in forty-one years, but while that makes for consistency, to a point, it doesn't amount to a direction. She shifted as a novelist, trying different things, but there was no pattern of evolution – except that the novels got longer, until the last. They did not get better. I'm not alone in thinking her most successful was *Under the Net*; it was also her first. Nor can it be said that Murdoch's two careers, as philosopher and novelist, merged happily. She resisted – I think rightly – any blurring of the lines between her often difficult work in philosophy and the 'innumerable intentions and charms' of fiction. It's not that Murdoch's life was incoherent –

though the web of her affairs isn't easy to unravel. But it didn't have the kind of narrative structure proponents of Life as Narrative approve, the sort that has 'an Agent, an Action, a Goal, a Setting, an Instrument – and Trouble'. Nor does Murdoch seem to have thought otherwise. Yet as I said in Chapter 1, I think she lived well enough. On the Life as Narrative view, a good life must form a coherent, linear story, one its subject tells herself. Murdoch is an exception to that – as are Strawson, Montaigne and Veeck.

In light of such examples, you may wonder why the view is so widely held. I think the answer turns on the amorphous open-endedness of storytelling. A question that is now overdue: what do the advocates of Life as Narrative mean by 'narrative', anyway? They gravitate to stories of the simplest and most linear form. 'For centuries there's been one path through fiction we're most likely to travel – one we're actually told to follow,' writes the critic and author Jane Alison in *Meander, Spiral, Explode*, 'and that's the dramatic arc: a situation arises, grows tense, reaches a peak, subsides.' It's in these terms that Life as Narrative is framed; they are what give it substance. The claim is that you should, and do, aspire to tell the story of your life as a single, integrated arc, 'something that swells and tautens until climax'. ('Bit masculo-sexual, no?' Alison jokes.)

As Alison observes, however, storytelling comes in countless forms, many of them non-linear. Stories meander, spiral, explode and branch, or divide into cells. Think of the telescoping pauses and prehistories of Prager on the Shot Heard 'Round the World, the repeated switchbacks and false starts. Or take Nicholson Baker's novella *The Mezzanine*, whose plot consists of a journey on an escalator during lunch hour, and whose interest lies in its delightful digressions, as the narrator reflects on shoe-laces, straws, deodorants, urinals, paper towels, childhood memories and escalators themselves. There are digressions within digressions, footnotes that run for paragraphs or pages in a masterpiece of storytelling that goes precisely nowhere.

If Life as Narrative meant only that there is value in seeing one's life as a story with one or more of these endlessly various forms, it would be harmless enough. Hence its air of plausibility. But in practice, Life as Narrative means a need for unity and linearity, for incidents that build to a fulfilling climax, won or lost; that's what its proponents demand. The prospect of stories like the ones I've just recounted undercuts their principal argument: that telling the story of one's life is a path to self-understanding and self-formation. Perhaps it is. But there are countless ways to make sense of yourself, even through stories, without picturing your decades as a quest. Why not bricolage, the character study, the riff?

What's more, there is a downside to unified, linear narrative: it is by squeezing your life into a single tube that you set yourself up for definitive failure. Projects fail and people fail in them. But we have come to speak as if a person can *be* a failure – as though failure were an identity, not an event. When you define your life by way of a single enterprise, a narrative arc, its outcome will come to define *you*.

It's a tendency we should fight. Whatever story you tell about yourself, however simple and straightforward, there is endlessly more to your actual life. As Joe Moran insists: 'To call any life a failure, or a success, is to miss the infinite granularity, the inexhaustible miscellany of all lives . . . A life can't really succeed or fail at all; it can only be lived.' The narrator of *The Mezzanine* is carrying a copy of *Meditations* by Marcus Aurelius, the Stoic philosopher who was emperor of Rome. At one point, he recalls a sentence he has read: 'Observe, in short, how transient and trivial is all mortal life; yesterday a drop of semen, tomorrow a handful of spice and ashes . . . Wrong, wrong, wrong! I thought. Destructive and unhelpful and misguided and completely untrue!' What makes the narrator's life worth living is not some grand narrative, running from conception or birth to inevitable death; it is the countless little thoughts and deeds and gentle, joking interactions that occupy day after day after day. If you pay attention, Baker intimates, there's enough in a single lunch hour to fill a book.

The more you appreciate the sheer abundance of incident, the more you'll see any life as an assortment of small successes and small failures, and the less prone you will be to say, despairingly, 'I'm a loser' – or with misplaced bravado, 'I'm a winner!' Don't let the lure of the dramatic arc distract you from the digressive amplitude of being alive.

The point is easy to misconstrue. Am I saying you should renounce ambition, not embark on projects that will structure decades of your life? Should you think small, kick back, relax? That is not what I'm saying and I would be a hypocrite if I was. I spent two decades of my own life striving for success in academia. I don't regret that. What I do regret is treating my life as a project to complete: first earn a PhD, then get a job; tenure and promotion; teach a class, publish an article, a book, then another and another and another – to what end? Life held only more of the achievements and frustrations of the past, a mere accumulation of deeds; and the present felt empty. That is why I had a midlife crisis.

It's not inevitable. By reflecting on the temporalities of action, one can learn how to pursue a project, even the most ambitious, without subverting one's life or seeing it solely in the glare of failure and success.

SOME YEARS AGO, I wrote an op-ed for *The New York Times* about the problem of 'living in the present'. We are often told to 'seize the day', but it would be wildly irresponsible to live like there's no tomorrow. That's a recipe for recklessness. What gives? I had an answer – in the form of a positive vision of living in the present – that appealed to ideas from Aristotle. Despite being warned not to read the comments when the op-ed went online, I was too curious to resist. What I encountered were furious Buddhists, livid that I would cite Aristotle, not Buddhism, in unleashing the power of now. My first reaction was defensive: when you have only a thousand words, you can't say everything; I'm not an expert on Buddhism; and the relationship between my view and Buddhist philosophy is complicated. My second reaction was that if Buddhism, for you, means leaving irate comments on op-ed articles, you may be doing it wrong.

My conception of living in the present turns on distinguishing two kinds of activity. On the one hand, there are projects to complete, activities that point towards a final state of failure or success. But there are also activities we don't complete, ones not defined by a terminal state – activities in which we don't succeed or fail. By focusing on the latter, we can make our lives less vulnerable to fate.

Similar ideas find expression not just in Aristotle but in Eastern philosophy, most explicitly the Bhagavad Gita, a Hindu scripture that dates from the second century BCE:

> motive should never be in the fruits of action,
> nor should you cling to inaction.
>
> Abiding in yoga, engage in actions!
> Let go of clinging, and let fulfillment
> and frustration be the same.

To explain what this could mean, and why it isn't exactly Buddhist, we'll turn to one of my favourite novels: *The Idiot*, written by Fyodor Dostoevsky over the course of a year, beginning in January 1868.

The history of *The Idiot*'s composition is not incidental here. In December 1867, Dostoevsky trashed what had been months of work on a projected novel about a criminal's moral conversion. His new plan was to write about '*a perfectly beautiful man*' – the Christ-like Prince Myshkin – throwing him into the chaotic, compromised world of contemporary Russia. He sent the first five chapters to his editor at *The Russian Messenger* on 5 January, followed by two more on the eleventh, and continued to write from instalment to instalment with no clear plan.

How do we know that there was no plan? In part because Dostoevsky says so in his notebooks; in part because he wrote the evidence of indecision into the text. Key ideas are introduced and then forgotten. In Part One, Myshkin is attributed the power to read people's characters in their handwriting. But he never goes on to use it. We are told that, as an 'invalid', he cannot marry. Yet he becomes romantically involved with two women and almost marries one of them. The later parts of *The Idiot* interpolate newspaper stories that Dostoevsky read months after he began to write. There is no way he could have planned around them – and he wants us to know it. The novel is as open-ended, unpredictable and ultimately sense-less as life itself. By the end, even the omniscient narrator gives up:

> Two weeks went by after the events recounted in the last chapter, and the position of the characters in our story changed so much that it is extremely difficult for us to set out on the continuation without special explanations. And yet we feel that we must limit ourselves to the simple statement of facts, as far as possible without special explanations, and for a very simple reason: because we ourselves, in many cases, have difficulty explaining what happened.

In the critic Gary Saul Morson's virtuoso reading of *The Idiot*, Dosto-evsky's aim was to write a novel that has no guiding structure at all. There is no linear arc, but nor does the story meander, spiral, radiate or branch. Its unity is the unity of Myshkin's character, a saint set down among sinners in situations that have no pattern or plan. Myshkin harbours no great ambition or urgent quest. He simply tries to do what is right in whatever circumstance he confronts. His intentions mostly fail: things rarely work out as he hoped they would.

For all that, Myshkin lives – as Dostoevsky meant him to – a beauti-ful life. He is not defined by his many failures. He is defined instead by his refusal to condemn the despised, his unerring modesty and truthfulness, his generosity, his will to believe and expect the best of others. Things do not turn out well for him. Myshkin is forced to betray one of the women he loves in order to save the other, who jilts him at the altar and is murdered by the man to whom she runs. But the fault is with the world. If Myshkin does not manage to live well, he responds as well as he can to dreadful events.

If someone called Myshkin a failure, they would not be wrong, exactly, but they would miss the point. That's not the way to think about his life. Myshkin cares about the struggle to do what is right as much as he cares about its outcome. Fittingly, this theme comes out in an extravagant digression: an hour-long speech by Ippolit Teréntyev, a nihilist who is dying of consumption; his 'confession' hinges on the life of Christopher Columbus:

> Oh, you may be sure that Columbus was happy not when he had discovered America, but when he was discovering it; you may be sure that the highest moment of his happiness was, perhaps, exactly three days before the discovery of the New World, when the mutinous crew in their despair almost turned the ship back to Europe, right around! The New World is not the point here, it can just as well perish . . . The point is in life, in life alone – in discovering it, constantly and eternally, and not at all in the discovery itself!

We find the same thought expressed in Dostoevsky's own voice, seven years later: '*Happiness lies not in happiness but only in the attempt to achieve it.*'

I would say: not happiness but living well, and not only but also. Prince Myshkin surely cares about the effects of his actions, what he actually achieves; but he cares, too, about the process of attempting to achieve it – about the journey, as much as the arrival. There is an insight here that lies between platitude and paradox, one that we can make precise with help from Aristotle.

In his *Metaphysics*, Aristotle contrasts two kinds of action. Some are 'incomplete', such as learning or building something, since 'if you are learning, you have not at the same time learned' and if you are still in the process of building, the structure is not yet built. Completion comes later, if at all. Then there is 'that sort of action to which . . . completion belongs' – meaning that it's never incomplete. An example of this is *thinking*: the moment you're thinking of Aristotle, you have already thought of him.

Aristotle calls activity of the first kind *kinêsis* and the second *energeia*. Stealing jargon from linguistics, we can say that building a house and learning the alphabet are 'telic' activities: they aim at terminal states, in which they are finished and thus exhausted. ('Telic' comes from the Greek word *telos* or end, the root of 'teleology'.) Walking home is telic: it's done when you get home. So are projects like getting married or having a child. These are things you can complete. Other activities are 'atelic': they do not aim at termination, a final state in which they have been achieved. While you are walking home, you are also walking, as you can walk with no particular destination. That is an atelic activity. So are parenting, spending time with friends and listening to music. You can stop doing these things, and you eventually will. But you cannot exhaust them. They have no limit, no outcome whose achievement brings them to an end.

We are always engaged in activities both telic and atelic. I am writing a book about the human condition – which I hope to finish – and I am thinking about the ways in which life is hard, an activity that has no end. You may be teaching your kid to tie their shoelaces – hoping they'll figure it out – but you are also parenting. The question is not which of the two you are doing but what you value. Dostoevsky's argument is that the value lies in atelic activities: in the process, not the project. That is what the Bhagavad Gita seems to say: 'motive should never be in the fruits of action' means 'do not invest in the completion of telic activities'; if one values only the process, one will still act but 'fulfillment / and frustration [will] be the same'. I think that goes too far: outcomes matter. Does your kid learn to tie their own laces? Does the doctor save a life? It makes a difference whether or not they do. Still, we are prone to care too much about telic activities – about the completion of projects – and to miss the value of the process. When we do that, we negate the present moment and set ourselves up to fail.

With telic activities, satisfaction is always in the future or the past. Your ambition is unfulfilled, and then it's over. Worse, your engagement with what you value is self-destructive. When you pursue a cherished goal, you aim to succeed, and so to end your engagement with something good. It's as though you're trying to destroy a source of meaning in your life. Meanwhile, it's projects like this that expose you to the risk of failure. You blow the interview for your dream job, mismanage your team, betray your ambition.

When you value the process, your relation to the present, and to failure, is quite different. Because they do not aim at terminal states, atelic activities are not exhaustible. Your engagement with them does not annihilate them. You can stop walking, or thinking, or talking to someone you love, but you can't exhaust those activities, leaving no more to be done. The other side of inexhaustibility is expressed by Aristotle when he insists, perhaps confusingly, on the 'completeness' of atelic activities: 'At the same time, one is seeing and has seen, is understanding and has understood, is thinking and has thought.' Atelic activities are realised in the present as much as they can ever be realised. If you value thinking and you are doing just that, you have what you value right now. Nothing you have done, or will do, can imperil this.

Aristotle's insight was that living well is atelic: 'But if you are learning, you have not at the same time learned, and if you are being cured you have not at the same time been cured. Someone, however, who is living well, has at the same time lived well.' Myshkin, for instance, whose failures are hedged by the fact that he is living as he should, whatever the results.

We should follow Myshkin, insuring ourselves against failure through the value of the atelic. There are parts of life in which projects play a secondary role. We don't spend time with those we love in order to divide the labour more efficiently as we cook, complete a puzzle more quickly or watch *Fleabag* on TV. We cook and do puzzles and watch TV together as a way of spending time with those we love. But even where projects loom large, as often in education and working life, in politics and society, chances are the process matters, too, unchained from failure or success. This value is easy to miss.

In early 1650, the Diggers' hopes for a communist future faltered. They had retreated to Cobham Heath where their homes were under threat of violence sanctioned by the New Model Army. Satellite colonies had been established in the Midlands and in Kent, but their survival was precarious. Gerrard Winstanley saw the writing on the wall. 'And here I end,' he wrote, 'having put my Arm as far as my strength will go to advance Righteousness: I have Writ, I have Acted, I have Peace: and now I must wait to see the Spirit do his own work in the hearts of others.' He went on to write a final book, *The Law of Freedom in a Platform*, which set out his vision for a new society, then lived out his days in peace. Winstanley may have been 'exhausted and bitterly disillusioned', in the words of Christopher Hill: a political failure. But generations have found value in his failed attempt, a struggle for equality from the ground up, celebrated by later socialists and memorialised in a folk song called 'The World Turned Upside Down'. After the 2016 US election, I listened obsessively to the British protest singer Billy Bragg, whose cover of the song, resolute and ringing, was the anchor of my soundtrack. Whatever Winstanley may have felt, his life was not a failure – not through posthumous success but because there is dignity in protest and protest is atelic.

In less exalted ways, the value of the process can insure us against failure. We only have to look for it, in atelic activities that matter to us – or correspond to projects that do. There is value in thinking through life's hardships even if this book is never published, value when a doctor struggles to save a life even if the patient dies. The insurance is not perfect. There is no way to eliminate failure in every form and no point pretending that results don't matter. But we can reframe how we live our lives so that our failures are less central.

The scope and limits of this shift in orientation – and its relation to Buddhist philosophy – are the subject of a classic film: the Bill Murray–Harold Ramis–Danny Rubin masterpiece, *Groundhog Day*. For those who do not know the plot, acerbic weatherman Phil Connors – played by Murray – is assigned to cover Groundhog Day in the Pennsylvania town of Punxsutawney. Each year, on 2 February, the groundhog Punxsutawney Phil is said to predict the weather: an early spring or six more weeks of winter, depending on whether or not he sees his shadow. It's as riveting as it sounds. Disaffected and eager to get home, Phil finds himself trapped in a time loop where every day is Groundhog Day. He repeats it with variations, first confused, then reckless, manic, suicidal and eventually serene. When Phil learns to accept his fate and to love the people around him, he is finally liberated. A new day dawns.

Critics agree that *Groundhog Day* is one of the great philosophical comedies, though they don't agree on what its philosophy is. One can read it as a meditation on the value of atelic activities. Phil can act, but nothing he does is ever really done: his actions produce no lasting change. They are erased as the day repeats. Is his life a test of the atelic orientation? Can process alone make human life good? But if it is a test, it's not a fair one. All sorts of atelic activities are unavailable to Phil. He can't spend time with friends outside of Punxsutawney, if he has them; nor can he explore the wider world. These facts remind us that while atelic activities are insulated from one kind of failure, they are not automatically available to us or easy to perform. We can fail to live well, even if the failure is not that of a project with a final end.

What's more, Phil *can* effect change, if only in himself. He remembers each day of his imprisonment and whatever he learns in the course of living it. By the time he is freed, Phil can play the piano, is fluent in French, has become an expert ice sculptor and knows how to flip a card into a hat from several feet. (How long did it take him to acquire these skills? According to Harold Ramis in the DVD commentary, Phil is trapped for a decade, but that is unrealistically brief. The most careful estimate puts his confinement at just under thirty-four years.)

Although Phil protests 'I am happy now', his life remains a kind of living hell. As I have acknowledged, projects matter, and if Phil's do not exactly fail, they never really succeed. An alternative reading of the film treats life in *Groundhog Day* as an allegory for samsara, the cycle of suffering conjectured by Buddhist philosophy, in which we live life after woeful life according to the law of karma. The goal is to be free of this cycle, no longer reborn, in the nothingness of nirvana. Thus Phil escapes from repetition to mortality.

Whatever its merits, the Buddhist interpretation of *Groundhog Day*, and of human life, is not the same as mine. For Buddhists, the power of now is about the transience and emptiness of reality, overcoming attachment to persons and things, the liberation of disengaging from what is fragile, perishable, shifting. For me, it's the opposite. To value the atelic is to attach oneself to the present. It's not about emptiness but fullness, not about detachment or liberation but engagement with, and attention to, what is happening now. Phil's life is impoverished in the loop: when it comes to actions that affect other people, he can't get anything done. But he can make the best of it, learning how to live a better life, one less mortgaged to success and failure, attuned not just to project but to process.

How can we make this transition ourselves? We may not be so lucky as to fall out of time, with thirty-four years to figure it out. And as I learned in midlife, you can't simply choose what you care about. I saw that two decades of academic striving had turned philosophy, for me, into a series of projects, each one painfully pursued or in the past. I had lost my love for philosophising with no end, atelically. That is why my days felt hollow and my future like a sprint to stay in place. But I couldn't just change. I had to work on myself and the work is still in progress. In *Midlife*, I wrote about meditation as a way to reorient oneself to the atelic. To focus mindfully on breathing, sitting, listening to sounds, detached from future goals is to learn to appreciate the present; it nurtures an ability to find atelic value that transmits into everyday life. I still believe all that. But I didn't say enough about the cultural forces that make it both urgent and difficult to transform ourselves. In that respect, I failed. As we will see, these forces are bound up with ones that reduce our worth to wealth.

THE IDEA THAT PEOPLE, not just projects, can be classified as failures has a history. In *Born Losers*, the historian Scott Sandage traces it back through the Great Depression to the mid-1800s, when 'failure' as a noun for people enters the dictionary. That one could not simply fail but be a failure was the upshot of social and economic changes. The US understood itself to be a land of entrepreneurs, the triumph of the businessman measured by high profits and good credit. Credit came to define Americans as individuals through the invention of the credit report. 'More than a bank balance or a character reference,' Sandage writes, 'a credit report folded morals, talents, finances, past performance, and future potential into one summary judgment . . . First-rate or third-rate, good as wheat or good for nothing, credit reports calibrated identity in the language of commodity.'

Add to this an individualist ethos in which success or failure in the market is attributed to the person, not to social circumstance. The essayist Ralph Waldo Emerson reflected on this attitude in 1860, noting: 'There is always a reason, in the man, for his good or bad fortune, and so in making money.' It was not just capitalists like Andrew Carnegie who fostered the belief that character is measured by success – as Carnegie preached in 'The Gospel of Wealth' in 1889. Thirty years earlier, Frederick Douglass, an abolitionist who was formerly enslaved, gave what was to be his most popular lecture, 'Self-Made Men'. 'I do not think much of the accident or good luck theory of self-made men,' he proclaimed. 'Opportunity is important but exertion is indispensable.'

> When we find a man who has ascended heights beyond
> ourselves . . . we may know that he has worked harder, better
> and more wisely than we. He was awake while we slept. He
> was busy while we were idle and was wisely improving his
> time and talents while we were wasting ours.

Allowing 'only ordinary ability and opportunity', he concludes, 'we may explain success mainly by one word and that word is WORK! WORK!! WORK!!! WORK!!!! . . . Give the negro fair play and let him alone. If he lives, well. If he dies, equally well. If he cannot stand up, let him fall down.'

The more one's life is understood in terms of a single enterprise in which one succeeds or fails on one's own merits, the more tempting it will be to identify as a loser or a winner, a failure or a success. Through the nineteenth century, Americans' self-worth was increasingly measured by prosperity. The financial panics that crashed the US economy engendered not just poverty and material hardship but spiritual collapse in those who failed. 'The land stinks with suicide,' Emerson wrote during the crash of 1837, as men who were unable to support themselves or their families took their own lives in shame.

The 'deaths of despair' recorded by economists Anne Case and Angus Deaton in present-day America thus have nineteenth-century precedents. These deaths are not explained by poverty alone. Since 2015, US life expectancy has fallen, and virtually all of the decrease is among non-college-educated Whites. Although they earn more on average than similarly qualified Blacks, they are 40 per cent more likely to die from suicide, alcohol abuse or overdose. Case and Deaton argue that the difference lies in the internalised belief that hard work yields success, in a refusal to admit systemic obstacles, and in a deficit of social solidarity. In other words, the explanation lies in seeing oneself, and not society, as a failure.

Black Americans are understandably more attuned to structures of injustice that impede prosperity. Some of these structures are historical, like the system of slavery Douglass railed against. Others are contemporary, like those anatomised, in part, by the writer Ta-Nehisi Coates:

> I came to see the streets and the schools as arms of the same
> beast . . . Fail in the streets and the crews would catch you
> slipping and take your body. Fail in the schools and you
> would be suspended and sent back to those same streets,
> where they would take your body. And I began to see these
> two arms in relation – those who failed in the schools
> justified their destruction in the streets. The society could
> say, 'He should have stayed in school,' and then wash its
> hands of him.

The language of 'personal responsibility' is a language of structural exoneration and self-blame. It turns away from patterns like the one described by Coates: from the 'school-to-prison pipeline', and the injustice and social waste of mass incarceration.

Behind these failures lies the power of the capitalist economy that drove rapacious colonial expansion and enslavement from the seventeenth century onwards – seeking new markets, new materials and captive labour – and which drives the contemporary decline of manufacturing in the West. The trend has not reversed; if anything, it's accelerated. Employment is increasingly polarised: the bad jobs get worse – more precarious, more consuming, less remunerative – while the best jobs get better; the middle evaporates. Economic inequality has soared. No wonder millennials spend more time on schoolwork than any generation before them: investment in their own 'human capital' seems like the only path through competitive college admissions to the dwindling supply of rewarding work. Life is a win-lose proposition and it is ever more perceived as one.

It is hard to know whether private ownership of the means to survival and flourishing can be reconciled with a world in which everyone's needs are met. Perhaps our only hope is to follow Winstanley and the Diggers, denying that Earth itself can ever be owned. (It is a puzzle, on reflection, how one could lay unqualified claim to land, or sea, or sky, whatever the needs of people to come.) But it is easy to see, and to say, that any programme of reform must speak not just to material need but to the ideology on which human worth is gauged by productivity, and productivity in terms of wealth. So long as self-esteem is tied to the production of market value, some will be 'failures', at best indebted for their living – through social insurance or a universal basic income – to the economic victories of others. The possessive individualism that portrays us as acquisitive social atoms may not be responsible for loneliness but it plays a critical role in the origins of failure.

This is no more than a chapter in the history of the telic mind-set under capitalism. Other chapters might explore the origins of the 'work ethic', how avarice was transformed from private sin to public good, or how economic relations that pit us against one another in a competition for primary goods conflict with social solidarity. These days, economic modes of thinking, structured by accumulation and repetition, infiltrate most parts of life. We count our online 'friends' and compete for 'likes' on social media, commodifying our relationships. A teenage love for philosophy becomes an adult obsession with climbing the rungs of the academic ladder, adding lines to a CV – no longer a means to philosophising but an end in itself. Mindfulness may be one way out: if not to throw the ladder away then to reframe it as the instrument it is. But it won't affect the roots of the ideology that shapes us – let alone the social and economic structures with which it's symbiotic.

Nor can we free ourselves from the myth that failure is our fault simply by observing when it's false. In the speech I quoted above, Douglass begins with a concession:

> Properly speaking, there are in the world no such men as
> self-made men. That term implies an individual independence
> of the past and present which can never exist.
>
> Our best and most valued acquisitions have been obtained
> either from our contemporaries or from those who have
> preceded us in the field of thought and discovery. We have all
> either begged, borrowed or stolen.

Yet he goes on to say what he says. Knowing that success turns on inequities of fortune that go beyond 'fair play' is not enough to shift its cultural meaning. As social animals, we care how we are perceived by those around us – as winners or as losers, say – and we can't just step outside society. Instead, we have to change it.

With failure, then, the personal is political. We have to acknowledge the structural causes of social and economic inequality and of our damaging self-conceptions. At the same time, I can hear a sceptical voice. It's easy to see how structures like these harm those of us perceived as losers. Those seen as winners may not care; and those who care may wonder what to do. How does injustice matter to the lives of those who are not directly subject to it? Remember Phil Connors, trapped in a temporal loop. What liberates him is only in part his orientation to the process; it's also his selflessness, his love and respect for others. Is there a lesson there for us?

Five

INJUSTICE

O n a typical evening in late 2020, I scan the headlines on my phone. Covid-19 has crashed the US economy. Millions are unemployed or forced to work in dangerous conditions, with or without health care. Meanwhile, the ultrarich get richer; the numbers in the headlines are so long I have to count the zeros. A handful of people make billions of dollars. Next, an article about the flood of repossessions that will come as pandemic benefits expire. When I click a link, it takes me to a story of political gridlock: Republicans refuse to vote on a bill that would extend existing aid. Click once more to read about threats of armed insurrection and civil war. If I click again, I can read about the faltering of democracy and the history of fascism. Or, for a change of subject, a Black man shot by police. Or a glacier melting so fast that scientists are stunned, a tropical storm, a wildfire, drought or floods, the harbingers of climate chaos. My heart begins to race with horror and panic.

I know that I am not alone. My experience is so common that it prompted the invention of new words: 'doomsurfing' and 'doomscrolling', an addiction to the limitless feed of awful news. As I force myself to put my phone away, I rage at the injustice of the world but feel powerless to change it. Perhaps you feel the same. We are not the first. Exiled from Germany to the US during World War II, the philosopher Theodor Adorno mourned: 'What would happiness be that was not measured by the immeasurable grief at what is? For the world is deeply ailing.' And yet what good does grieving do? It's enough to make one envy those who do not care, who close their eyes to oppression, inequity, war. If I cannot save the world, maybe I should save myself.

The circumstance is new, but the question is old: why concern oneself with justice when solidarity brings pain? It's a question Plato asked in the *Republic*, whose second book begins with the mother of all thought experiments. The *Republic* is a dialogue between Socrates and a variety of interlocutors who question the value of justice. One of them is Glaucon – in real life, Plato's older brother. He tells the story of a shepherd stumbling on the body of a giant in a chasm opened by an earthquake. On the giant's finger, the shepherd finds a golden ring that has the power to make its wearer invisible. 'When he realized this,' Glaucon owns, 'he at once arranged to become one of the messengers sent to report to the king. And when he arrived there, he seduced the king's wife, attacked the king with her help, killed him, and took over the kingdom.' Easier said than done, one might think. But in Glaucon's jaded view, it's what we'd all attempt:

> Now, no one, it seems, would be so incorruptible that he
> would stay on the path of justice or stay away from other

people's property, when he could take whatever he wanted
from the marketplace with impunity, go into people's houses
and have sex with anyone he wished, kill or release from
prison anyone he wished, and do all the other things that
would make him like a god among humans. Rather his actions
would be in no way different from those of an unjust person,
and both would follow the same path.

We care about justice, or pretend to care, only because we are afraid of being caught.

As psychological conjectures go, this one is tenuous at best. Its only support is Glaucon's cynicism. Realistically, different people would employ the power to be invisible in different ways. Asking what *you* would do is a fun philosophical icebreaker. But the ring has come to stand for a dilemma: when self-interest and morality conflict, why not simply do what's best for you? If you would profit from a life of crime, so what if it's morally wrong? And if concern for justice brings 'immeasurable grief', wouldn't it be better not to care?

When we think about injustice in our own lives, or in the lives of others, the first step to clarity is seeing that these questions are confused. The philosopher Ludwig Wittgenstein believed that this was true of all philosophical questions. 'Philosophy is a battle against the bewitchment of our intelligence by means of language,' he wrote. All too often, the con comes at the start: 'The decisive movement in the conjuring trick has been made, and it was the very one that we thought quite innocent.' Here the trick is to oppose morality and self-interest without explaining what 'self-interest' means. If it means happiness, the mood or feeling – a happy state of mind – then yes, it may conflict with due concern for others' rights and needs. Those who care may be distressed at the state of the world; while the unjust may be happy. But happiness is not the only thing worth wanting. At the beginning of this book, we pictured Maya, plugged into an artful simulation, unaware that everyone she meets and most of what she seems to do and know is fake. Maya is happy, but she does not live well; she hardly lives at all. Suppose, then, that the object of self-interest is not happiness but human flourishing: we want our own lives to be good. But part of living well is living as we should, feeling what there is reason to feel and doing what there is reason to do. If there is reason to care about the rights and needs of others, it follows that we cannot live our own lives well without concern for them. Self-interest and morality agree.

It doesn't follow from this that there *is* good reason to care about the rights and needs of others, or that they have rights against us at all. If there is and they do, morality is part of living well; if there's not or they don't, morality is a fraud. Either way, the question is not what to do when morality and self-interest come apart but how we should respond to the injustice of the world. What does it mean to live well in a time of sustained oppression, inequity or war? To answer that question, I'll turn to the life and work of a moral saint.

THERE ARE SOME who take the fact of suffering hard. Born in Paris on 3 February 1909, the philosopher Simone Weil lived to see her homeland under German occupation during World War II. Escaping with her parents to New York City before heading to London alone, she ate only the rations allowed in occupied France. It was a form of solidarity she had practised all her life. 'When she learned that soldiers at the front during the First World War were being denied their ration of sweets,' her biographer Palle Yourgrau writes, 'young Simone abstained from chocolate.' She was less than ten years old. Teaching in France two decades later, Weil would give her salary to needy workers, refuse to heat her apartment when the unemployed could not afford to heat their own, and insist on doing factory and farm work that harrowed her frail physique. She would labour until shattered, unable to meet the pace of factory production lines. At the vineyard where she worked eight hours a day, she 'was often too tired to keep standing, and so continued to pick grapes lying down . . . she milked cows at dawn, peeled vegetables and, as always, helped the local children with their homework'. Weil died eventually of starvation, maintaining her self-imposed ration while suffering from tuberculosis in a sanatorium in Kent, on 24 August 1943. She did not complain. 'What a beautiful room in which to die,' she had said of the place where her life would end.

There is a terrible logic to Weil's self-sacrifice. It wasn't fair that she should eat while others starve, and since she could not feed them, she would starve herself. The principle is one she had framed in high school, in an essay written for 'Alain' – a pen name for Émile-Auguste Chartier – the teacher of Raymond Aron, Simone de Beauvoir and others. Weil recounts the story of Alexander the Great crossing the desert with his army in 325 BCE. When his soldiers brought him water in an upturned helmet,

Alexander poured it out onto the sands. If he had drunk the water, Weil writes, 'Alexander's well-being . . . would have separated him from his soldiers . . . Every saint has poured out the water; every saint has rejected all well-being that would separate him from the suffering of men.'

There is an otherworldliness to Weil, a near-inhuman obstinacy. She was nicknamed '*La Trollesse*' by her family, 'the Martian' by Alain, by others 'the Red Virgin' and 'the Categorical Imperative in skirts'. (The Categorical Imperative was Immanuel Kant's strict formulation of the moral law.) Trapped in London in 1942, Weil campaigned for a squadron of nurses to be air-dropped at the front lines of the war; she would lead them herself. 'The project may appear impracticable at first sight,' Weil grants, 'because of its novelty.' But she was deadly serious.

Raised as a secular Jew, Weil went on to have profound experiences of Christ, first while visiting Assisi in 1937, then at the Benedictine abbey of Solesmes the following year. She was always heretical, unable to accept the violence of the Old Testament God or a religion that would damn the unbeliever. While Weil saw God in Christ, she refused to see him only there: 'We do not know for certain that there have not been incarnations previous to that of Jesus, and that Osiris in Egypt, Krishna in India were not of that number.'

Even as she glimpsed another world, the mystical Weil was an incisive critic of ours. While studying philosophy at the selective École Normale Supérieure – Weil came first in the entrance exam in 1928; the philosopher Simone de Beauvoir was second – Weil helped to found a school for the education of railroad workers. Weil took part in marches and strikes; she met with and criticised Leon Trotsky; she campaigned against fascists in the Spanish Civil War. Weil wrote about the role of violence, not just economic force, in the oppression of workers. She recognised the power of propaganda and warned against the misuse of language to set us against one another. Weil found a place for philosophy here: 'To clarify thought, to discredit the intrinsically meaningless words, and to define the use of others by precise analysis – to do this, strange though it may appear, might be a way of saving human lives.'

If there are models of what it would be to take injustice and human suffering seriously, to make no excuse for oneself, there is none better than Simone Weil. The problem is that her model is terrifying. Inspiring, yes, but terrifying, too. I couldn't do with my life what Weil did with hers; who among us could? If that is what it means to care about injustice, maybe I don't care, after all. Maybe I shouldn't.

It is doubts like these that bring us to philosophy, searching for an argument to prove that we should care. Philosophers have done their best. In the *Republic*, Plato argued that there is no prospect of psychic health without a kind of justice in the soul, and that we cannot be unjust to others if we're just within ourselves. Two thousand years later, Immanuel Kant would claim that we cannot be truly free without conforming to the moral law, treating others not just as means but ends. But the proofs don't work. You cannot argue an egomaniac into caring about others. There's no internal contradiction in the view that we should each pursue our own happiness, regardless of the rest. Attempting to reason someone out of that position is like trying to dissuade a committed conspiracy theorist or debating a sceptic who believes that the apparent world is fake. They won't accept the premise of any argument that would refute their view.

This is not because they are right but because we've been tricked again. It's one thing to know that a conspiracy is false or that our world is real. It's another to persuade someone who's determined to think otherwise. We asked if we should care about injustice and by sleight of mind the conjurer flipped the question – can we prove to *him* that we should care? – without our noticing the difference. We can know that justice matters without being able to convert an obdurate sceptic. That's not what ethics is about. As Weil sardonically observes:

> A man who is tempted to keep a deposit for himself [when it belongs to someone else] will not keep from doing it simply because he has read [Kant's] *Critique of Practical Reason*; he will refrain from it, because it will seem to him, despite himself, that something in the deposit itself cries out to be given back.

If justice doesn't cry out to you already, reading Kant is unlikely to help.

What is the alternative to argument? Attention, or close reading. For Weil, 'reading' is a metaphor for the interpretive work we constantly do as we confront the world and measure our response to it. 'Thus at each instant of our life,' she writes, 'we are gripped from the outside, as it were, by meanings that we ourselves read in appearances . . . The sky, the sea, the sun, the stars, human beings, everything that surrounds us is in the same way something that we read.' Reading is automatic, then; but reading well is hard.

Think back to Bartleby, the scrivener, whom we abandoned in Chapter 1, preferring not to leave his office, or to work, or to eat, or to do much of anything at all. What is the meaning of this enigma? Interpreting 'Bartleby' – like interpreting Bartleby – is a treacherous business. There are as many readings of Melville's story as there have been readers: Bartleby as Melville, refusing to write what pays; Bartleby as existentialist; as nihilist; as transcendentalist; as alienated worker; as activist or protestor; and more. Bartleby is caught up in a ruthless system of repetitive, meaningless drudgery that turns copyists like him into 'human Xerox machines'. But the most empathic book about the story, Dan McCall's *The Silence of Bartleby*, is a rebuke to every critic who treats Bartleby as a symbol: this 'does him great violence – it takes his silence away from him'. I'll try not to do that, even as I recruit poor Bartleby, sublimely taciturn, to my argument.

Bartleby's best reader is the lawyer who narrates his story. Melville's narrator has been denounced by critics as a symbol of capitalist exploitation, blind to Bartleby's humanity. But those who treat the lawyer in this way do him violence – they take his volubility away from him. If the lawyer struggles to see Bartleby's humanity, it's also true that he keeps struggling. Refusing the skeletal vocabulary of preference – Bartleby 'prefers not to' – the lawyer tries again and again to take in Bartleby with words: 'I can see that figure now,' he writes, 'pallidly neat, pitiably respectable, incurably forlorn! It was Bartleby.' As the lawyer flounders in the face of his recalcitrant employee, the compound expressions keep coming. There is Bartleby's 'cadaverously gentlemanly *nonchalance*', his 'impotent rebellion . . . mild effrontery . . . wonderful mildness . . . miserable friendlessness . . . pallid haughtiness . . . austere reserve . . . tame compliance'. Bartleby is 'singularly sedate' and 'singularly mild'.

I'm not saying that the lawyer takes the measure of Bartleby; he can't. Attempting to grasp Bartleby in words is like trying to wrap one's arms around a ghost. The lawyer ends up clutching at himself. But he is trying to do justice to a flesh-and-blood human being, to tell the truths that will tell him what to do. That the lawyer is so patient with Bartleby, that he offers Bartleby his home: these facts can't be detached from the generous humility of his diction.

Melville's lawyer reminds me of the mother, known only as 'M', in a thought experiment due to Iris Murdoch. M finds her daughter-in-law, D, 'pert and familiar, insufficiently ceremonious, brusque, sometimes positively rude, always tiresomely juvenile' – but slowly works to see through her prejudice 'until gradually her vision . . . alters': 'D is discovered to be not vulgar but refreshingly simple, not undignified but spontaneous, not noisy but gay, not tiresomely juvenile but delightfully youthful, and so on.' In shifting her perceptions, Murdoch argues, the mother may be coming to the truth. Not 'impersonal quasi-scientific knowledge of the ordinary world, whatever that may be, but . . . a refined and honest perception of what is really the case . . . which is the result not simply of opening one's eyes but of a certain perfectly familiar kind of moral discipline'.

This is what Murdoch and Weil mean by 'attention'. What moves us ethically, first, is not reasoning but an effort to appreciate what's there. I'm sure more people go vegan after reading descriptions or seeing images of factory farms than on the basis of the arguments – maybe good ones – that come later. The same is true of human suffering and injustice. I don't need arguments to make me flinch as I read the headlines on my phone. I only need to take them in – not just as bits of information, clicks, but as a testament to the lives of others. As Murdoch wrote: 'The more the separateness and differentness of other people is realized, and the fact seen that another man has needs and wishes as demanding as one's own, the harder it becomes to treat a person as a thing.' This is not just speculation. In an extraordinary study of altruism, the political psychologist Kristen Monroe explored the motivation of people who help strangers at great risk to themselves: 'Altruists see the world differently,' she confirmed. 'Their behavior results from the recognition . . . that the needy person is human and therefore entitled to certain treatment. Humanity plus need: This is the only moral reasoning, the only calculus for altruism.'

The challenge is to maintain this vision, not to turn away from those around us or treat the headlines as empty words. Reflecting on the difficulty of compassion, Weil warned: 'Thought flies from affliction as promptly and irresistibly as an animal flies from death.' I let my eyes skip over the news, scrolling away, surfing on the crest, not swimming in the deep. In my troubles, I forget that every person I encounter suffers troubles of their own, as urgent and as real as mine. That's why the book you're reading now, though it has been about afflictions in my life and yours, can serve a moral purpose, too. In thinking about the hardships of human life, I have been thinking about myself, but I can't help thinking of others, the profusion of humanity whose adversities I don't face.

There's the depth of physical pain, the possibility of compassion for one's past and future self and so for other people. There's the challenge of adapting to disability, too often frustrated by prejudice and poor accommodations. And there's the need for attachment, thwarted in isolation and grief, that displays the dignity of human life. Love is, we found, a moral emotion: you do not really love someone unless you see a value in them that would survive the loss of love. They would matter even without you; and since anyone can be loved, the same is true of every human being.

Both Weil and Murdoch drew a line from attention to unconditional love. 'Among human beings,' Weil wrote, 'only the existence of those we love is fully recognized.' 'Friendship has something universal about it. It consists of loving a human being as we should like to be able to love each soul in particular of all those who go to make up the human race.' For Murdoch: 'Love is the perception of individuals. Love is the extremely difficult realization that something other than oneself is real.' What matters here is less the plea for universal love than its continuity with respect. The value we seek out in love is the value that injustice violates. Justice and love are not two unrelated virtues – like truth and beauty – but different aspects of one good: the lower bound of what we owe to one another and the limit at which our lives converge.

What makes both love and justice hard is, in part, the urge to flee from suffering and 'the fat relentless ego' Murdoch finds inside us all. But there are outward obstacles, too, ideologies that distort the social world and prevent us from seeing what's there. (For instance: the ideology on which life is defined by projects and every person is a failure or success.) Philosophy cannot prove that we should care about others when we don't, but it can help us to articulate injustice and uncover what it calls on us to do.

This is where argument comes in, but not just argument, also clarity of thought – Weil's war against propaganda – and conceptual upheaval. In Murdoch's words, 'The task of moral philosophers [is] to extend, as poets may extend, the limits of language, and enable it to illuminate regions which were formerly dark.' The darkness we confront is the injustice of the world and the sense that we are powerless to change it. Can philosophy shed some light?

THOUGH IT BEGINS with justice as a trait disdained by Glaucon's invisible shepherd, Plato's *Republic* veers abruptly into politics. The bulk of the dialogue portrays the constitution of Plato's utopia, the *kallipolis* or beautiful city. In it, each citizen is assigned for life to one of three castes: philosopher-guardians who rule the city, auxiliary guardians who protect it, and producers who work to meet the city's material needs. The guardians have no private property and the family is abolished, with children being raised in common. The justice of the city lies in everyone doing the job they are assigned.

Not surprisingly, few subsequent philosophers accept this Platonic ordinance, with its oppressive regime of mandated work and communal parenting. But they have often shared Plato's ambition: to describe a social order that is perfectly just. This aim survived, through many ups and downs, into the work of John Rawls, the political philosopher who revitalised the field with *A Theory of Justice* in 1971. For Rawls, political philosophy begins with 'ideal theory', the description of a fully just society, governed by 'strict compliance' – meaning everyone conforms to the principles of justice – with a sufficiency of material goods. Rawls called this a 'realistic utopia', taking 'men as they are' and 'laws as they might be'. Utopia in hand, we turn to 'non-ideal theory', which speaks to the conditions we are actually in. It tells us to strive for utopia by the most effective means morality permits.

As you might expect from the premise of this book, I don't believe political philosophy should start with a vision of perfect justice, any more than ethics should begin with Aristotle's ideal life. We don't need a blueprint for utopia to identify injustice in the world. Just look at America's past and present: the dispossession and killing of indigenous peoples, chattel slavery, the failures of Reconstruction, Jim Crow laws, redlining, mass imprisonment, police brutality, voter suppression. We can perceive injustice here without the help of ideal theory; and ideal theory does not point the way to its repair. By its nature, ideal theory abstracts from structures of oppression; at its worst, it obfuscates them. (Utopia does not see race.)

It's doubtful, anyway, that we are in a position to conceive an ideal world. One of the insights of the 'Critical Theory' developed by Frankfurt School philosophers in the mid-twentieth century is that ideology distorts our sense of what is humanly possible. To take just one example: it is hard not to see the technological automation of work – self-driving cars, mechanised warehouses, computerised data entry – as a threat to employment that will leave millions destitute, not as the liberating prospect of freedom from toil. This is not just realism, a concession to what is politically feasible now. It is backed by the ideology of productive labour as a source of self-esteem – forgetting that this connection may be produced by the economic system it is used to justify. Would 'unemployment' feel like failure if no one needed to work? I'm not saying that it wouldn't. I'm saying it's impossible to know what human life would be – how we might relate to work and one another – under social arrangements radically different from those we've encountered so far.

Political philosophy should not theorise perfect justice, then: we have no way of picturing an ideal world. Instead, it should help us see what's wrong with the world around us and what we must do to change it. The Critical Theorist Theodor Adorno saw political philosophy this way. In the fragments he collected as *Minima Moralia* and published in the aftermath of World War II, Adorno refused to dream of 'an emancipated society' or 'the fulfilment of human possibilities'. We cannot aim at emancipation now, Adorno held, since we do not know what words like these could mean. Reading human potential from the wreckage of human history is like studying botany with one's specimens in parched soil. One can tell that they lack water, but not what they will look like when they flower. For Adorno, there 'is tenderness only in the coarsest demand: that no-one shall go hungry any more'. If we can't conceive utopia, at least we can respond to unmet needs.

In its moral clarity, this demand gets something right; but it misses something, too. It's reminiscent of the fashion for 'effective altruism', the idea that whatever we do to help those in need, we should do it by the most efficient means. Effective altruists like William MacAskill and Peter Singer argue that the affluent should do more to help those who are badly off. Specifically, they argue that we should donate money to the most effective charities, and they devote considerable acumen to rating this effectiveness by dollars per 'quality-adjusted life years' saved. (Mosquito nets and malaria medicines come first.) Effective altruists have been criticised for neglecting politics, ignoring the social causes of poverty and human suffering: political solutions are hard to quantify. But they also neglect the question of responsibility. Effective altruists treat every need alike; but some weigh on us more heavily than others. Our moral relation to human suffering is more urgent when we're caught up in its causes than when they have nothing to do with us.

Philosophers can help us think through these entanglements. Thus, Iris Marion Young, a pioneering political theorist who died of cancer at the age of fifty-seven, developed the idea of 'structural injustice' – injustice that is not localised in unjust attitudes or actions but emerges interactively – and proposed a 'social connection model' of responsibility. These are concepts with which to light the dark.

When injustice is structural, it is created or sustained, at least in part, by practices that don't depend on prejudice or on particular unjust acts. Even if no one held sexist views about women's abilities or denied them employment because they are women, for instance, the gendered division of labour in which women do the majority of unpaid childcare and domestic work would systematically disadvantage them. The injustice would not lie in any given attitude or act of exclusion but in our collective expectations. It is essentially structural.

Young contends that we're responsible for structural injustice. At the root of her argument is a contrast between culpability or blame and responsibility for change. To take another example: while it's unfair to criticise present-day Americans for our nation's racist history, we are often implicated in systems that sustain its legacy now. Consider education: American cities are de facto segregated and since schools are supported by local taxes and Black communities are disproportionately poor, their schools are on average less well funded than schools in wealthy neighbourhoods. Equality of educational opportunity is a myth. While the structures are not my fault, I was caught up in them when I bought a home in Brookline, Massachusetts, partly for the excellent public schools. 'The social connection model of responsibility says that individuals bear responsibility for structural injustice,' Young writes, 'because they contribute by their actions to the processes that produce unjust outcomes.' She is looking at me.

Young's point is not about guilt or shame but the obligation to work for change. This is what she means by 'responsibility'. I may not be wrong to want a good education for my child, or be to blame for the way schools are funded, but I should advocate for reforms that redress the injustice to which I contribute. We can extend Young's model not just to those who participate in social practices that perpetuate injustice but to those who benefit from an unjust past, as many Americans benefit from a history of colonial expropriation and slavery that in part explains the huge disparity in median wealth between White families (a median of roughly $188,000) and Black ones (around $24,000). Data on indigenous people is scarce, but a 2000 survey put the median net worth of a Native American individual at $5,700; this had declined from 1996. We needn't be to blame for these disparities to profit from them and so to be the beneficiaries of injustice.

In the face of such realities, what are we to do? 'The almost insoluble task,' Adorno wrote, 'is to let neither the power of others, nor our own powerlessness, stupefy us.' Young's argument is that our accountability 'is not primarily backward-looking, as the attribution of guilt or fault is'. It's a matter not of blame but of political agency: 'Taking responsibility for structural injustice . . . involves joining with others to organize collective action to reform the structures.' The obligation is daunting, Young admits: 'If I share responsibility . . . for every social injustice that results from structural processes to which I contribute by my actions, then this makes me responsible in relation to a great deal. That is a paralyzing thought.' But the proper response to paralysis is not inaction; it is to take the first step. Do one thing.

Let me admit – or rather, insist – that I am not a model to emulate here. I have not done much: occasional marches and political campaigns, voting regularly, talking politics with friends – none of it likely to make much difference. Young confronts bystanders like me with what the political philosopher Ben Laurence calls 'the question of the agent of change'. It's not enough to identify injustice, nor to vote for politicians you prefer, who will often be indifferent or obstructive to the change you want to see; and it is typically futile to act alone. Our task is to find collective agents – movements, unions, interest groups – that have the power and will to make things happen.

I am not much of an activist, let alone a leader, and I feel routinely overwhelmed by the injustice of the world. If that resonates with you, my advice is to pick a single issue and find a group that you can join. For me, the issue was climate change and the group was Fossil Free MIT.

The ethics of climate change is sometimes framed as a matter of beneficence towards the future: leaving a good-enough world for those to come. In fact, it raises issues of injustice, past and present. The storms and floods and droughts, the crop failures, water shortages and refugee crises that climate change brings will be much worse in parts of the world that have done little to cause the problem. Earth is already 1.1°C (2°F) warmer than it was in 1850. At 2°C (3.6°F), which we are on pace to hit in thirty years, a million people in Bangladesh will be permanently displaced by rising oceans. Central Africa will lose 10 to 20 per cent of its rainfall; when combined with hotter temperatures, the effect will be catastrophic. Meanwhile, hundreds of millions of people in south and central Asia will lose fresh water as mountain glaciers vanish. Beyond 2°C (3.6°F), the effects will be more brutal. Yet more than half of the emissions responsible for climate change are due to countries in the developed world that will be spared the worst. If we restrict our horizon to 1990 – the last date at which one could claim ignorance with any shred of plausibility – the US and Europe account for more than 25 per cent of emissions, China for 15 per cent. And if we limit ourselves to current emissions, the US remains at nearly 12 per cent with less than 5 per cent of the world's population. Meanwhile, in sub-Saharan Africa, per capita emissions are one twentieth of those in the US.

To cause substantial harm to others for one's own benefit is as clear an injustice as there can be. It's what Glaucon's shepherd does when he becomes invisible: he kills the king and takes the throne. I live in a nation whose policies have subsidised the harms of climate change and which has taken few serious steps to mitigate or prevent those harms. Like everyone, I am enmeshed in the fossil fuel economy. I am responsible for this injustice as participant and beneficiary, and so obligated to act. For most of my life, I did little or nothing: I couldn't see how, though I didn't look too hard. I worried a bit about my carbon footprint. There's nothing wrong with that, but it has little to do with the kind of collective action required to make a difference. In 2007, a class at MIT worked out the carbon footprint of a homeless person in the US, living off the grid but relying on infrastructure that depends on fossil fuels; it was still ten times that of someone living in sub-Saharan Africa. The problem is systemic. It is not an accident that the idea of obsessing about one's individual carbon footprint was aggressively promoted by British Petroleum – a way to divert attention from corporate blame.

Things began to change for me in 2014, when I moved to MIT. I arrived on a campus adorned with what seemed to be contemporary art: four miles of blue caution tape stretched across the exterior walls of buildings and landscapes. The tape varied in height, always a few feet from the ground, dipping near my ankles at times, surging to my waist as I walked towards my office, slashing its way across doors and windows. A closer look revealed a message printed on the tape: 'Global Warming Flood Level – Tell MIT: Divest from Fossil Fuels'. Placed by the Fossil Free student group, the blue tape marked the level to which floods would rise on campus in a five-foot storm surge – like the one that hit Boston in 2012 – under sea levels projected for 2050. MIT would be engulfed.

In the wake of the installation, the students forced a year-long Climate Change Conversation, sponsored by the Institute, in which a committee of students, faculty and administrators would formulate policy proposals. One focus was divestment: withdrawing MIT's $18 billion endowment from investments in fossil fuel companies. Financial boycotts have played a historic role in pressuring the recalcitrant, from the sugar boycotts that helped end British slavery to the divestment campaign against apartheid in South Africa. The committee voted 9 to 3 that MIT should divest from coal and tar sands, the most environmentally damaging forms of fossil fuel extraction, and there was unanimous support for an Ethics Advisory Council to review the allocation of MIT's endowment.

With the students, I watched, dismayed, as the summer passed and MIT announced – having consulted with the 'Corporation', MIT's Board of Trustees – that its first-ever Climate Action Plan would ignore the recommendations of its own committee. (David Koch, perhaps the most ruthless opponent of US climate legislation, was then a lifetime member of the MIT Corporation and one of MIT's most generous donors.) There would be no divestment and no ethics.

That was the point at which I got more seriously involved, helping to organise a faculty protest of the decision and supporting the students who occupied the hallway outside the president's office, demanding more. The students took the lead; with other staff, I followed, providing food and moral support. The sit-in was threadbare at times, with just a few warm bodies in the corridor, but it lasted four long months, through spring 2016, and in the end there were concessions. Not divestment, but an advisory committee to track the progress of MIT's strategy of 'engagement' with fossil fuel companies and a forum to address the ethics of climate change. It was not ideal. But as we pass the six-year mark, a new student group, MIT Divest, is putting pressure on the administration once again.

I tell this story not because it is a narrative of success – or of failure, for that matter – but because it illustrates the need for an agent of change. I overcame my inertia because I found a focus for collective action with a realistic chance to make a difference. MIT could not ignore the students: if nothing else, the publicity would not be good. It's because of the students that we have a Climate Action Plan at all. Though it didn't turn out as I had hoped, my participation was the closest I have come to meeting the responsibility for justice anatomised by Iris Marion Young.

I SAID THAT I AM NOT a model and that continues to be true. Since 2015, I have given talks on climate justice here and there and addressed the issue online. Three years ago, I developed a class on the ethics of climate change with a colleague at MIT. I am sure it is not enough. What is the use of teaching climate ethics? To raise awareness, maybe – though why take the class unless you already care? More to build community and to deepen understanding of the problems we confront. My hope is that the students I teach will go on to meet the responsibilities I won't. There is a fair amount of guilt that I am not doing more.

You may share that guilty feeling, directed at the issues that disturb you most: mass incarceration, poverty, voting, civil rights. Are we doing all we can to fight injustice? It's a question for everyone, but for philosophers like me it takes a particular form, eliciting old debates about theory and practice. Karl Marx is famous for his eleventh thesis on Ludwig Feuerbach (a German philosopher and anthropologist): 'The philosophers have only interpreted the world, in various ways; the point is to change it.' Ben Laurence ends his essay on the agent of change with the fear that 'academia divides the philosopher from many agents of change, especially where such agents suffer from serious injustice and oppression'. This fear is epitomised in the life and work of Theodor Adorno.

Born in Frankfurt in 1903, Adorno was the son of a wine merchant; his mother had been a professional singer. Adorno himself was something of a prodigy, playing Beethoven piano pieces by the age of twelve. He went on to study composition with Alban Berg. But he made his mark with the Critical Theorists of the Frankfurt School, exposing ideologies that frustrate human flourishing. As a Jew in Germany, Adorno was denied the right to teach in 1932. He left for Oxford two years later, studying with the British philosopher Gilbert Ryle. It was at Oxford that Adorno wrote a polemic against jazz music, published under the appropriate pseudonym Hektor Rottweiler. He was not a fan of pop culture.

Adorno moved to New York City in 1938 and then to Los Angeles, a home he shared with other German émigrés, including the playwright Bertolt Brecht, the novelist Thomas Mann and the composer Arnold Schoenberg, in what was nicknamed 'Weimar on the Pacific'. In America, Adorno wrote several of the books for which he is best known: *Dialectic of Enlightenment* (with fellow Critical Theorist Max Horkheimer), *Philosophy of New Music* and *Minima Moralia*. Adorno returned to Frankfurt in 1949 and lived there until his death twenty years later, completing two masterpieces: *Negative Dialectics* and *Aesthetic Theory*.

Adorno matters here because he was a trenchant critic of industrial capitalism, influenced by Marx, who more or less gave up on constructive political engagement. Adorno is unremittingly, sometimes comically, negative. In *Minima Moralia*, he reads, at times, like a mash-up of philosophical guru and grouchy uncle, dispensing acid remarks about the trivia of contemporary life. 'We are forgetting how to give presents,' he writes at one point:

> Real giving had its joy in imagining the joy of the receiver.
> It means choosing, expending time, going out of one's way,
> thinking of the other as a subject: the opposite of distraction.
> Just this hardly anyone is now able to do. At the best they give
> what they would have liked themselves, only a few degrees
> worse.

The pretext for such gripes is a disturbing vision of the world: 'What the philosophers once knew as life has become the sphere of private existence and now of mere consumption, dragged along as an appendage of the process of material production, without autonomy or substance of its own.' The living dead, we have no prospect of flourishing.

Adorno saw the German revolution fail at the end of World War I. A socialist uprising led by workers who had fought in the war, the revolution dissipated in a year, quelled by the centrist coalition of the Weimar Republic. If the proletariat could not play the transformative role that Marx envisaged, Adorno feared, then there is no agent of change. There is nothing to do but retreat to the academy and to map the contradictions of society until circumstances shift. Adorno's contemporary György Lukács scorned this act of withdrawal: 'A considerable part of the leading German intelligentsia, including Adorno,' he wrote, 'have taken up residence in the "Grand Hotel Abyss" . . . a beautiful hotel, equipped with every comfort, on the edge of an abyss, of nothingness, of absurdity.'

Lukács had a point. As student protests hit Frankfurt in 1968, Adorno called the police to have the students arrested. The students responded by interrupting his classes, demanding an apology. The disruption peaked when female protestors 'surrounded him on the platform, bared their breasts and scattered rose and tulip petals over him'. Adorno cancelled the lecture and fled. When students became activists – as Angela Davis did when she joined the Black Panthers, returning to the US from Frankfurt in 1967 – Adorno dismissed their efforts. 'He suggested that my desire to work directly in the radical movements of that period was akin to a media studies scholar deciding to become a radio technician,' Davis would later write. She went on to become a philosophy professor, an agitator who was one of the FBI's ten most wanted, and a prescient critic of the prison-industrial complex.

For me, Adorno is a cautionary tale: a brilliant thinker who convinced himself that teaching and writing were a substitute for resistance. It's an occupational hazard in academia, a kind of intellectual bad faith. Even when our work has real effects, as it sometimes does, we can always do more to meet the responsibility for justice. The same is true of anyone: who can say they do enough?

Adorno can instruct us here. What drives his pessimism, his withdrawal, is the belief that – in the words of *Minima Moralia* – 'wrong life cannot be lived rightly'. He meant that we cannot live well in conditions of injustice that sully every aspect of social life; we cannot even know what flourishing would be. But there is a more mundane truth in his aphorism. We know that there are limits to what we can ask of ourselves in living rightly, given who we are. Not all of us – perhaps none of us – can be Simone Weil. How we are capable of living turns on our psychology and social circumstance, our partial grasp of the social world, the need to maintain our equilibrium and to meet our obligations to kith and kin. (There are difficult questions here about what can be asked of those subjected to injustice, for whom survival may be challenging enough.) But though we know that we have limits, we don't know where those limits are. The result is that, when I ask myself whether I am doing enough to meet my responsibility for justice, it would be an awfully neat coincidence if the answer were yes. What are the odds that I've hit the mark precisely, the most I can expect of myself? Close to zero, I would think. The result is that I am virtually certain that I am falling short. Perhaps it's obvious that I am. But the same reasoning applies to almost anyone, even those who do much more, people whose lives are devoted to social change. They can't be sure they've done enough. In conditions of profound injustice, we are compelled to doubt that we are living well.

There's instruction and reassurance to be found in this. We shouldn't feel too bad that we feel bad: our guilt is not a mistake. More important, we shouldn't let it put us off, condemning our own efforts as too small. They may be small – but it's perverse to deal with that by throwing up our hands and doing less. There is value in a single step towards justice, and one step leads to another. While it's hard to make a difference on one's own, the march of millions is made up of individuals; and there's collective action at every scale, from local unions to protests and political campaigns.

Confronted with the scope of human misery, some despair: 'It doesn't matter what I do,' they say, 'since millions will still suffer.' But this thought is confused. You may not do enough, but the difference you make when you save a life is the same whether you save one of two or one of two million. A protest may not change the world, but it adds its fraction to the odds of change. It's wrong to disregard the increments. We make the same mistake when we deny ourselves compassion, knowing that others suffer more. 'It may be the most important lesson I ever learned,' the poet Richard Hugo wrote, 'maybe the most important lesson one can teach. You are someone and you have a right to your life.' You have a right to your suffering, too.

There is a final theme on which I empathise with Adorno, which is his deep attachment to both art and abstract thought. Perhaps it was wrong of him to retreat to the Grand Hotel Abyss, listening to Beethoven's late quartets, when he could have supported the students in Frankfurt. No doubt Adorno was mistaken about jazz. But he was right to resist what we might call 'the tyranny of the ameliorative': the feeling that, in times of crisis, all that is worth doing is to fight injustice, so as to make things less bad than they are. How can we listen to music, or work on the more speculative questions of philosophy and science, while the planet burns? But while political action is urgent, it's not the only thing that matters.

In fact, it couldn't be. If the best we could do was to minimise injustice and human suffering, so that life was not positively bad, there would be no point in living life at all. If human life is not a mistake, there must be things that matter not because they solve a problem or address a need that we would rather do without but because they make life positively good.

They would have what I've called 'existential value'. Art, pure science, theoretical philosophy: they have value of this kind. But so do mundane activities like telling funny stories, amateur painting, swimming or sailing, carpentry or cooking, playing games with family and friends – what the philosopher Zena Hitz has called 'the little human things'. It's not just that we need them in order to recharge so that we can get back to work, but that they are the point of being alive. A future without art or science or philosophy, or the little human things, would be utterly bleak. Since they will not survive unless we nurture them, that is our responsibility, too.

When the two Simones – Weil and Beauvoir – met at long last in the courtyard of the Sorbonne, Weil told her namesake that nothing matters but the revolution that will feed the poor. Beauvoir replied that we should also care about life's meaning. Weil's brusque retort: 'It's clear you've never gone hungry.' Though Weil had the final word, Beauvoir was right. When I think about the horrors of climate change, part of what disturbs me is the suffering of millions in storms and floods, droughts and famines, but part is the prospect of cultural devastation. I think of the history that will drown, the traditions that will starve, the impoverishment of art and science and philosophy. That is not a world in which we can be at home. If we cannot see our way to a better future, what meaning can we find in life today?

Six

ABSURDITY

I became a philosopher at the age of seven or eight, soon after scribbling that lonely verse in a vacant playground. But it wasn't loneliness that made me philosophical. It was a sense of wonder, and an undertow of worry. I remember staring at the corrugated trunks of trees in the playground at break, stunned by the fact that there was anything at all. The thought that there might not have been induced a lurch of anxiety I now recognise as Jean-Paul Sartre's 'nausea': alarm at the brute facticity of things, their sheer contingency, their blank resistance to reason. What if everything ceased to be? Why shouldn't it?

By coincidence – or fate – the protagonist of *La Nausée*, Sartre's existentialist fiction, is upset by tree trunks, too. 'Never, until these last few days, had I understood the meaning of "existence",' he confides.

> Existence everywhere, infinitely, in excess, for ever and
> everywhere; existence – which is limited only by

existence . . . At any instant I expected to see the tree-trunks shrivel like weary wands, crumple up, fall on the ground in a soft, folded, black heap. *They did not want* to exist, only they could not help themselves. So they quietly minded their own business; the sap rose up slowly through the structure, half reluctant, and the roots sank slowly into the earth.

Reality is astoundingly, disturbingly gratuitous.

Wonder and worry, anxiety and awe: these feelings are what led me to philosophy, aimed less at tree trunks than the totality of existence. 'Why is there something rather than nothing?' asked the polymath Gottfried Wilhelm Leibniz in the early eighteenth century. The American philosopher Sidney Morgenbesser may have had the best response: 'If there were nothing, you'd still complain!' It's an impossible question, but that doesn't prevent us from asking it.

The question of absurdity is not about explanation but about meaning. Yet it comes from the same perspective: one in which we meditate on the universe and on the place of humanity within it, the course of human history little more than the blink of a cosmic eye. The absurdity of life has become a cliché. Picture Earth as filmed from space, our blue marble spinning through the dark; imagine as the shot pulls back to show the solar system, Earth shrinking in the distance, then our galaxy of a hundred billion stars, most of it empty space, one of billions in the universe, expanding over billions of years. How minute and insignificant we seem in the vast, unfathomed reach of space and time. How preposterous that we take ourselves so seriously. Who has not felt, at times, the sheer absurdity of things?

We should deal with these emotions. The feeling of absurdity is disquieting in itself; but it speaks to the place of other hardships in human life. Exploring absurdity leads us back to love and loss, to narrative and the non-ideal, to acknowledgement and attention. We'll find our way through the absurd by staring into the void – reflecting on the prospect of human extinction. We'll take on the injustice of the world. And in the midst of absurdity, we'll uncover the meaning of life. To say that life has meaning is to say that it is not absurd. We need to ask what that could mean.

THAT PHILOSOPHERS PONDER the meaning of life is as much of a cliché as life's absurdity. When I risk admitting to a stranger that I teach philosophy for a living, I am sometimes asked the ultimate question: 'Tell me, what does it all mean?' I have a canned response: 'We figured that out in the 1950s, but we have to keep it secret or we'd be out of a job; I could tell you, but then I'd have to kill you.' In fact, academic philosophers rarely consider the question, and when they do, they often dismiss it as nonsense.

There is no question that the question is obscure. 'What is the meaning of life?' we ask, and wonder what we're asking. The extent to which the question is neglected can be hidden by well-meaning substitution. Thus philosophers ask what it takes for someone to live a 'meaningful life'. That is the topic of *Meaning in Life and Why It Matters*, an accessible, enlightening book by the philosopher Susan Wolf. Wolf is representative both in shifting the question – from the meaning of life as a whole to individual lives – and in the outline of her answer. According to Wolf, to live a meaningful life is to engage, more or less happily and successfully, in activities that matter. That might involve relationships with other people, caring for those you love; it might be the pursuit of justice; it could be art or science or philosophy, productive work or joyful leisure.

The philosophical threat here comes from nihilism: the idea that nothing matters. In his 'Confession', the novelist Leo Tolstoy gave elegant expression to this threat, describing an existential crisis. 'My life came to a standstill,' he wrote. 'I could breathe, eat, drink and sleep and I could not help breathing, eating, drinking and sleeping; but there was no life in me because I had no desires whose gratification I would have deemed it reasonable to fulfill.' Nihilism is a form of philosophical scepticism, and like the sceptic we met in the previous chapter, who denied that other people matter, the nihilist cannot be refuted on their own terms. You can't show that anything matters if you don't assume that something does. If you try to argue with a nihilist, you'll stall. As before, that doesn't mean the nihilist or the sceptic has it right or that we don't know that they're wrong. It means that what illuminates our world with value, first, is not an argument; it's attention.

The thing to notice, anyway, is that the question of life's meaning is different from the question how to live a meaningful life. For Wolf, as for her fellow travellers, some people's lives are meaningful while others' lives are not. The meaning that interests her is a personal possession.

Gerrard Winstanley lived a meaningful life; so did Iris Murdoch and Bill Veeck. Bartleby, the scrivener, did not. But when we ask if life as a whole has meaning, we are not asking for something that varies from life to life. The question of absurdity has one answer for everyone or it has no answer at all. What is the meaning of human life, as such?

It is this question philosophers are prone to dismiss, finding it nonsensical. The sticking point is 'meaning'. What on Earth does that word mean in 'the meaning of life'? We talk about the meaning of words or linguistic meaning, the meaning of an utterance or of writing in a book. When we ask for the meaning of life, are we asking whether life has meaning in this sense? Could human life be a sentence in some cosmic language? I suppose it could. There could be alien beings who communicate through the activities of species over centuries, for whom revolutions are commas and stretches of progress or regress make up words. They might chance upon a text spelled out by accident in human history, like the text of *Hamlet* hammered out by monkeys at typewriters. That would be an astonishing fact. I'd be curious to know what we happen to say. But it's not the meaning we are looking for. To be unwitting ink in some alien script would only confirm our absurdity. It might tell us what human life means for aliens, but not what it means for us.

Maybe we shouldn't be hung up on 'meaning'. What about the point or purpose of life? Humanity could play a role, or have a function, in a larger system. In Douglas Adams's *Hitchhiker's* books, Earth is part of a galactic computer designed, ironically, to find the Ultimate Question of Life, the Universe, and Everything. (Notoriously, the answer is '42'.) But if we were cogs in a cosmic machine, discovering our function wouldn't tell us what life means. It would leave our existential maladies untouched. The philosopher Thomas Nagel makes a grisly version of this point:

> If we learned that we were being raised to provide food for
> other creatures fond of human flesh, who planned to turn us
> into cutlets before we got too stringy – even if we learned that
> the human race had been developed by animal breeders
> precisely for this purpose – that would still not give our lives
> meaning.

You might think that the problem is with the function. 'Admittedly, the usual form of service to a higher being is different from this,' Nagel concedes. 'One is supposed to behold and partake of the glory of God, for example, in a way in which chickens do not share in the glory of coq au vin.' True enough. But this doesn't help us understand our question. The point remains that function alone is not enough to give life meaning, not in the sense that interests us – which means that 'meaning' in 'the meaning of life' does not mean function.

It is here that philosophers tend to throw in the towel. Remember Wittgenstein on 'the bewitchment of our intelligence by means of language'. Perhaps we've been bewitched by words and the problem of absurdity will vanish when we see that the question of life's meaning is not meaningful. (Or maybe that makes things worse? What could be more absurd than finding that one's deepest question has no meaning?) This time around, though, I am not convinced. No matter how elusive it may be, the question doesn't fade; it whispers quietly in our minds. What is the meaning of life? We will get somewhere, at last, by going right back to the start.

'Since the dawn of time,' the sophomoric essayist declares, 'humanity has pondered the meaning of life.' Except we haven't. The question doesn't come up in Plato or Aristotle, Seneca or Epictetus, Augustine or Aquinas, Descartes, Hume or Kant. They ask what it means to live a good human life; but they don't ask what life means.

'The meaning of life' – that turn of phrase – originates in 1834. It appears in the mouth of a fictional philosopher, Diogenes Teufelsdröckh ('God-born devil's-dung'), in the British writer Thomas Carlyle's parodic novel *Sartor Resartus*. According to Teufelsdröckh, the world we sense is but the outer clothing of God or Spirit: 'Thus in this one pregnant subject of CLOTHES, rightly understood, is included all that men have thought, dreamed, done, and been: the whole external Universe and what it holds is but Clothing; and the essence of all Science lies in the PHILOSOPHY OF CLOTHES.' It's hard to know how to take the extended joke, which sets the stage for serious despair. In a chapter called 'The Everlasting No', Teufelsdröckh laments his isolation from the world around him: 'To me the Universe was all void of Life, of Purpose, of Volition, even of Hostility: it was one huge, dead, immeasurable Steam-engine, rolling on, in its dead indifference, to grind me limb from limb.' It is in this mood that he questions the meaning of life – and coins a phrase.

There are two clues for us in this. First, the question of life's meaning was more or less invisible until the nineteenth century. Second, it's a question that we ask in times of emptiness or anguish, when life feels meaningless or absurd. We ask it when we suffer or grieve without consolation, when we are lonely and bitter, when misery and injustice overwhelm us. Life is profoundly flawed. Is there some meaning to it all? The question is pressing for us, as it was for early existentialists like Søren Kierkegaard, tormented by the angst of human existence, when we fear that it means nothing.

What is 'meaning' in 'the meaning of life'? When we look for the meaning of a work of art, a narrative or a painting or a piece of music, we are interested not in its linguistic meaning – except in the case of verbal narrative, there may not be any – and not in its purpose or function in a system. What we want is its significance. We want a description of what it does and how – what it is 'about' in the broadest sense – that tells us what our attitude towards it ought to be. We are looking for truths that will tell us how to feel. (The answer is often complex and multivalent.) Interpretation here unites attention, explanation and affect. So it is with the meaning of life. The question is how to feel about everything, about the whole of existence and the place of humankind within it. The meaning of life would be a truth about us and about the world that answers that question: a truth that tells us what to feel and why. That is why we ask the question when life is hard. We want to be reconciled, somehow, to loss and failure, injustice and human suffering. We are hoping for a truth that will take the edge off our despair.

This interpretation helps explain the timing of the question, why it should materialise at the point in history that it did. Before the nineteenth century, the vast majority of people took for granted a religious worldview that prescribed an answer. 'Religion, whatever it is, is a man's total reaction upon life,' wrote the psychologist William James in *The Varieties of Religious Experience*, published in 1902. 'To get at [this reaction] you must go behind the foreground of existence and reach down to that curious sense of the whole residual cosmos as an everlasting presence, intimate or alien, terrible or amusing, lovable or odious, which in some degree every one possesses.' When one inhabits a religion, one's total reaction is positive, or if not positive, then reconciled or redeemed. Religions offer saving visions of the whole residual cosmos. If they do not proclaim the meaning of life, they offer the conviction that there is one, however inscrutable it may be. There is a truth that tells us how to feel.

Albert Einstein went further, asserting that any answer to the question 'What is the meaning of human life, or of organic life altogether? . . . implies a religion.' The problem for me, as for the existentialists, is how to sustain the meaning of life when a religious worldview is not a given. If God is dead, is human life absurd?

THE FIRST THING TO SAY is that not all religions appeal to God. Beside the monotheistic religions – Judaism, Christianity, Islam – there are polytheistic religions like Hinduism, and religions that are non-theistic, like Buddhism. It's not easy to say what these religions have in common, what makes them religions, binding together a 'total reaction upon life' with creeds and doctrines, rituals and practices. But one element of any religion is belief, or faith, in something that transcends the ordinary world – if not

God or gods then a metaphysics of some kind, as in the Buddhist doctrine of emptiness and the puzzling proposition that there is no self.

Religion is, I believe, essentially metaphysical. It provides a picture of the world as a whole that guides our total reaction: how we are meant to feel about life, the universe, and everything. This might involve our relation to God or it might not; but it always involves a metaphysics of transcendence. Take Buddhism, for instance. What distinguishes Buddhist meditation from mindfulness as a method of stress control is the aim of ending suffering through discovering the truth – in particular, the truth that you don't exist. If neither you nor those you love are real in anything like the way you once believed, mortality and loss are less traumatic. (That is the idea, anyway; it's never been clear to me why discovering this 'truth' is not at least as traumatic, like being told that everyone you know, including you, is already dead.) To come to terms with life through meditation for serenity, or through talk therapy, is not to be religious, or to know the meaning of life, since it is not to discover any such truth.

For many religions, the meaning of life appears in a theodicy that vindicates the ways of God to man. Life is hard, but there's a story to be told on which it works out for the best, perhaps in some immortal afterlife. If we are not given the story, we have faith that it exists, beyond our comprehension. Thus the poet Alexander Pope ends the first epistle of his 1734 *Essay on Man*:

> All Nature is but Art, unknown to thee;
> All Chance, Direction, which thou canst not see;

All Discord, Harmony, not understood;

All partial Evil, universal Good:

And, spite of Pride, in erring Reason's spite,

One truth is clear, 'Whatever IS, is RIGHT.'

Pope's rhyming, repetitive antitheses instruct us that every harm is secretly beneficial, every complaint has a rejoinder, theodicy like clockwork, the tick-tock of God's design, invisible to us, underscored at last by the insistence of 'IS, is'.

Modern philosophers detached the aim of theodicy – showing that whatever is, is right – from the dogmas of traditional religion. Thus Leibniz would argue, on logical grounds, that this is the best of all possible worlds. Jean-Jacques Rousseau would trace the ills of human life to the depredations of society: they are within our power to fix. And for Georg Wilhelm Friedrich Hegel, writing in 1837, the 'insight to which philosophy ought to lead . . . is that the real world is as it ought to be'.

If the meaning of life can survive without God, and without traditional religion, perhaps there is hope for atheists like me. What we need are truths about the world, and the place of humanity in it, that tell us how to feel about the whole residual cosmos – ideally, ones that help us come to terms with suffering and injustice. Sounds good, except it is a mystery what these truths could be. According to William James, the New England transcendentalist Margaret Fuller told Thomas Carlyle, who coined 'the meaning of life': 'I accept the universe.' Carlyle was not impressed: What else are you supposed to do? A more common reaction is scepticism.

Once we set aside theodicy, as I did at the start of this book, what truths could redeem the suffering we don't deserve or repair the rife injustice of the world? How can we accept the universe?

Worse, why should we believe that there is any way we ought to feel, that reality dictates our total reaction to life? James is, once more, a plausible spokesman:

> It is notorious that facts are compatible with opposite
> emotional comments, since the same fact will inspire entirely
> different feelings in different persons, and at different times
> in the same person; and there is no rationally deducible
> connection between any outer fact and the sentiments it
> may happen to provoke.

It is not news that different temperaments respond in different ways to misery and vice. The pre-Socratic philosopher Democritus found reality so preposterous that he could not help but laugh; his predecessor Heraclitus wept. This was back in the fifth century BCE.

Perhaps the most likeable response to the threat of indeterminacy is Frank Ramsey's. Ramsey was a prodigy who died of a liver infection in 1930 at the age of twenty-six, having done extraordinary work in mathematics, economics and philosophy. Soon after his twenty-second birthday, Ramsey was invited to speak about the meaning of it all. 'Where I seem to differ from some of my friends,' he said, 'is in attaching little importance to physical size.'

I don't feel the least humble before the vastness of the
heavens. The stars may be large but they cannot think or love;
and these are qualities that impress me far more than size
does. I take no credit for weighing nearly seventeen stone . . .
[Humanity] I find interesting and on the whole admirable. I
find, just now at least, the world a pleasant and exciting place.
You may find it depressing; I am sorry for you, and you
despise me. But I have reason; and you have none; you
would only have a reason for despising me if your feeling
corresponded to the fact in a way mine didn't. But neither can
correspond to the fact. The fact is not in itself good or bad; it
is just that it thrills me but depresses you. On the other hand,
I pity you with reason, because it is pleasanter to be thrilled
than to be depressed, and not merely pleasanter but better for
all one's activities.

The best we can do, for Ramsey, is to take a positive attitude on pragmatic
grounds: always look on the bright side of life. It would be less pleasant
but no less accurate to view the whole world with dismay. This is the absurdity of life.

Although the tone is different, it is the same absurdity that fuels *The
Myth of Sisyphus*, in which the French philosopher Albert Camus wrote:
'Man stands face to face with the irrational. He feels within him his longing for happiness and for reason. The absurd is born of this confrontation
between human need and the unreasonable silence of the world.' The

absurdity is not that the world dictates a negative response, that the truth is terrible, but that the most profound of questions – 'What is the meaning of life?' – receives no answer. There's no particular way we ought to feel about the world: when it comes down to it, our total reaction is arbitrary. We ask; and the universe shrugs. Is there nothing left to say?

IN THE SPIRIT OF ABSURDITY, I'll argue that the question of life's meaning *can* be answered by considering that the answer might be grim.

In *Children of Men*, a novel by P. D. James adapted for film by Alfonso Cuarón, humanity has become sterile. No child has been conceived for eighteen years. Futureless, society shudders towards collapse. But James is interested less in the practical challenges of the final generation – who will take care of the elderly? what happens to the global economy when we can't invest in or borrow against the future? – than in their spiritual life. How would you feel if you knew that humankind would not go on? In the world of the novel, protagonist Theo Faron writes that 'those who lived gave way to [an] almost universal negativism, what the French named *ennui universel*'.

> It came upon us like an insidious disease; indeed, it was a
> disease, with its soon-familiar symptoms of lassitude,
> depression, ill-defined malaise, a readiness to give way to
> minor infections, a perpetual disabling headache. I fought
> against it, as did many others . . . The weapons I fight with are
> my consolations: books, music, food, wine, nature . . . [But]

> without the hope of posterity, for our race if not for ourselves,
> without the assurance that we being dead yet live, all pleasures
> of the mind and senses sometimes seem to me no more than
> pathetic and crumbling defences shored up against our ruins.

James was anticipated by the anti-war activist and writer Jonathan Schell in *The Fate of the Earth*, an influential work of speculative non-fiction that appeared in 1982. Though his ultimate topic is nuclear apocalypse, Schell pulls apart its elements: the painful, premature death of billions and 'the cancellation of all future generations of human beings'. Like James, he imagines the second without the first, through general sterility; and like James, he expects a bleak response. To those who face extinction, he writes, 'the futility of all the activities of the common world – of marriage, of politics, of the arts, of learning, and, for that matter, of war – would be driven home inexorably'.

Thirty years after Schell, and twenty years after James, the American philosopher Samuel Scheffler put the infertility scenario to philosophical use. Like James and Schell, he writes, 'I find it plausible to suppose that such a world would be a world characterized by widespread apathy, anomie, and despair; by the erosion of social institutions and social solidarity; by the deterioration of the physical environment; and by a pervasive loss of conviction about the value or point of many activities.' In ways we barely recognise and rarely explore, the meaning of what we do from day to day depends on an implicit faith that humanity will outlive us, at least for several generations. It depends, as Scheffler puts it, on our belief in a 'collective afterlife'.

When you imagine yourself in the infertility scenario, how do you respond? With horror, grief, malaise? Does the bustle of daily life lose its significance for you? That our activities are mortgaged to the future may be obvious when their outcome is long distant – as when we contribute incrementally to a cure for cancer that may not be discovered for decades – but the phenomenon is arguably more pervasive. At least part of the point of art and science is lost if they will have no audience in fifty years. Why bother to contribute to traditions that are doomed? If humanity is sterile, there will be no children to carry our collective inheritance onwards. Even the transient pleasures of reading or listening to music, of eating and drinking, may pall, as they do for Theo Faron, to whom 'pleasure now comes so rarely and, when it does, is indistinguishable from pain'.

Should one despair in the face of human extinction, as Faron does? Should one respond instead with equanimity? Or is it all a matter of temperament, depressing to some, perhaps, but anodyne to others? Is there a way one *ought* to feel about the whole residual cosmos in *Children of Men*?

I believe there is. Our emotions here are not purely subjective, any more than they are in grief or love. Thus there are good reasons to resist Faron's nihilistic response. For one thing, it isn't clear *why* the value of reading or listening to music, let alone of food and drink – a value that seems contained in the moment of engagement – should depend on what is to come. It's not like curing cancer in a hundred years. Even as the world ends, we can cling to the solace of art and the pleasures of the flesh.

What's more, there's a question of time. Why should the value of what we do evaporate in the heat of imminent extinction, when we knew all along that humanity's days were numbered? Scheffler dubs this 'the Alvy

Singer problem', after the nine-year-old in Woody Allen's *Annie Hall* who sees no point in doing homework if the universe will one day end. Alvy's stance may seem ridiculous, but there's an argument behind it. If the value of what we do rests on the flourishing of subsequent generations, then the final generation, whenever it comes, does nothing of value. It cannot flourish. But then the same is true of the penultimate generation, by the very same principle, and so of the generation before that. The dominoes of flourishing cascade from human extinction to the present, leaving only worthless debris.

Unless you're prepared to believe that nothing we do matters, you can't believe that of the final generation. And while we cannot prove that there is value in the world – at least, not to the nihilist's satisfaction – that doesn't mean it isn't true. Faron may be so depressed he doesn't want to listen to opera, read P. G. Wodehouse novels or play board games with close friends; but those activities are still worthwhile. Their value does not rest entirely on posterity. (Why should it?) It follows that the very first domino need not fall. Even the final generation can find value in their lives.

We shouldn't overstate the impact of extinction, then. But I don't think we should celebrate it, either. Since the 1990s, a handful of extreme environmentalists have advocated voluntary human extinction: let us cease to reproduce for the sake of the planet. But even they see our extinction as a loss – a noble sacrifice – and they'd prefer a world in which we manage to survive in harmony with nature. They just don't think it's going to happen.

All of which helps us to push back against the cliché of absurdity. Here the news is perversely good. Since there are reasons for responding to the end of human history in one way, not another, our total reaction need not be arbitrary: some attitudes are more rational than others. We shouldn't welcome imminent extinction; but we shouldn't let it lead us into nihilism. Reality *can* dictate how we should feel about existence as a whole. In other words, life could have meaning. As potential meanings go, the ones elicited by extinction are dismaying – so negative they hardly count. But once we measure our response to the infertility scenario, we can vary the hypothetical, testing our total reaction, asking what the facts tell us to feel. This could mean giving arguments – like the arguments I gave against Theo Faron – but mostly it's description, not unlike the description of other people that directs our moral lives.

Why feel sorrow at the imminent extinction of humanity? In part because we value human history and its subject, humankind, and in valuing them, want them to go on. Scientists talk about 'ecological grief', as those on the front lines of the climate crisis see ecosystems collapse and endangered species die. They are never coming back. Like grief at the sheer loss of life, ecological grief is about the irreplaceability of what is lost; it's a basic expression of love. Humanity is lovable, too, for all its frailty. Grief at the prospect of human extinction is the reflexive form of ecological grief. If we love humanity, we'll want it to survive.

But mere survival is not enough. Our emotions should be focused less on preservation than on change; for we have unfinished business. Think about injustice, with which we struggled in Chapter 5. Add to that our ignorance, how much we still don't know about the universe, the yet-unanswered questions of pure science and philosophy. Add, too, our untapped creativity and our inhibited capacity for love, including love of the natural world. For human life to end like this would be – in a sense that is not just metaphorical – premature.

It would be different if, in the course of generations, humanity worked to mitigate injustice, to protect the vulnerable and to answer human need. Imagine we achieved a kind of society unimaginable now: that we came as close to justice as human frailty permits. Not utopia, but the best that we can do. Sterility might still afflict us, as it does in *Children of Men*, but we'd answer with invention, solidarity and compassion. We'd find ways to care for one another, to share art and friendship, the solace and companionship of whistling in the dark. We would meet our end with grace.

I'm not saying I'd be happy with this narrative, but I think it's one we can accept. If humanity went extinct this way, I'd be okay with that. After all, as Alvy Singer knew, we are bound to go extinct one day. The change is not in outward circumstance, but in us: how we collectively respond to the adversities we face. What would be terrible is for human history to end – a history of prejudice, slavery, misogyny, colonial violence, war, oppression and inequality, along with fitful progress – with our potential so far from being realised. I'm not saying that the future can redeem the past, that if we made society more just that fact would compensate, somehow, for the injustice we've already done. The past can't be erased. But for that very reason, all we can aspire to do is mend the future.

Justice matters, then, not only for its own sake but as an antidote to absurdity. Other things matter, too: the relationships and pastimes, work and play, that make for meaningful lives. But human existence as a whole would not have meaning if the good things in it were distributed in ways that are perpetually unjust. To overcome injustice is to forge a truth that tells us how to feel, and so give meaning to life.

Thus the existentialists were wrong: reason may dictate a total reaction to the world, and that reaction may be, if not exactly affirmation, then acceptance of the universe and the place of human life within it. This need not rest on anything transcendent or divine, the non-existence of the self or the immortality of the soul. The afterlife it calls for is collective. The meaning of life – the truth that tells us how to feel about the whole residual cosmos – would lie in our halting, perhaps perpetual, progress towards justice in this world.

This vision is less distant from religion than it seems. It is often said that religious belief originates in fear of death, that it's meant to console us in our mortality. But that view is simplistic. As the pioneering theologian John Bowker argued, the ubiquitous injustice of our world – where the innocent suffer and the guilty go free – cries out for metaphysical solution. That is why religions look for justice in a world beyond, or dismiss the world we know as an illusion. The truth would otherwise be intolerable. The point of being immortal is not simply to cheat death but to make room for the justice our mortality frustrates. The virtuous must be rewarded and the vicious damned; and if that does not happen in this world, it must happen in another. Justice comes first – as it does in my account of the meaning of life.

I don't believe in another world, not one that compensates for ours. If there is meaning to be found, we must find it in the shape of history, the arc of the moral universe that bends, or does not bend, towards justice. This way of understanding human history, and its relation to the future, was conceived soon after the Enlightenment, around the same time as 'the meaning of life'. For Hegel, history is the intelligible process of 'spirit' striving towards self-consciousness and human freedom. For Marx, on a standard reading, it is the inexorable sequence of economic modes by which primitive communism gives way to agriculture, to feudalism, to capitalism, and eventually to the higher communism whose banner reads 'From each according to his ability, to each according to his needs!' The catch is that Hegel and Marx, like religious eschatologists, regard the direction of human history as determined in advance. There is a final state to which we are inevitably progressing. I don't believe that's true. The arc of the moral universe depends on what we do and that depends on us.

I am not by nature optimistic. When I look at where we are heading, I am terrified, by climate change most of all. It is not only that it's causing, and will increasingly precipitate, sweeping, unjust harm but that progress on every aspect of injustice – social and economic inequality, violence and exclusion, the faltering of democracy – turns on weathering the storm. If climate change leads to widespread food and water insecurity, mass migration, conflict and war, we can forget about equality and human rights.

That climate change threatens the meaning of life is not mere rhetoric; it is plain fact. Human life *could* have meaning. Its meaning could be to limp slowly, painfully, contingently towards a justice that repairs, so far as it can, the atrocities of the past. If human history had that shape, we should accept it and play our part. In our small corner of the vast, indifferent cosmos, we would have made a home. If climate change leads instead to social collapse, that meaning will be lost, not in absurdity but in shame.

In his essay 'On the Concept of History', the Frankfurt School philosopher Walter Benjamin – Adorno's friend and colleague – refused to portray the past in progressive terms. It appears to the 'angel of history', he wrote, as a 'single catastrophe which keeps piling wreckage upon wreckage and hurls it in front of his feet. The angel would like to stay, awaken the dead, and make whole what has been smashed.' But in Benjamin's prophetic image, 'a storm is blowing [that] propels him into the future', and he cannot stop to repair the damage: 'This storm is what we call progress.' It is for us to interrupt the storm, taking hold of the present to give meaning to the past. In his notes for the essay on history, Benjamin employed another apt analogy: the steam engine. 'Marx says that revolutions are the locomotive of world history,' he wrote. 'But perhaps it is quite otherwise. Perhaps revolutions are an attempt by the passengers on the train – namely, the human race – to activate the emergency brake.'

Our task now is to pull the emergency brake on climate change – along with the injustice, domestic and global, gendered and racial, with which it is entwined. Our efforts will shape the facts that tell us how to feel. We'll rise to the challenge or we won't. Things may look bad, but remember how they looked before, when we faced the vacuum of absurdity. The question of life's meaning is intelligible and the answer is up to us.

Today, the future is uncertain. We can't be sure, can hardly guess, how history's arc will bend. And so we cannot say what human life means, if it means anything at all. The question that remains is what to feel when so much is unknown. What total reaction makes sense when the meaning of life is unsettled and at risk? Should we be lifted by hope or flattened by despair?

Seven

HOPE

One of my philosophical heroes is Diogenes the Cynic, an adversary of Plato in ancient Greece. Diogenes was funny. When he heard Plato's account of man as the featherless biped, Diogenes showed up at the door of the Academy brandishing a plucked chicken, declaring 'Here is Plato's man!' For Diogenes, philosophy was a performance art, something to be lived, not just discussed. Diogenes was principled. Dismissing Plato's dialogues as 'a waste of time', he showed his faith in practice over theory, and in virtue over wealth, by living in a storage jar in the streets of Athens. He carried a lamp with which he professed to search, without success, for an authentic human being. Diogenes was inspiring. He was a political revolutionary, a 'citizen of the world' who dreamed of an equality unimagined in his time. 'When asked what is most precious in life, [Diogenes] said: "Hope."'

The idea that hope is empowering, noble, even audacious, has become conventional wisdom. But it was not always so. To explain why hope deserves a chapter in this book, an entry in the catalogue of human hardships, we need to go back to Pandora's box – in fact, another jar – and to the Greek poet Hesiod, four hundred years before Plato.

A contemporary of Homer writing in the eighth century BCE, Hesiod tells the story of Prometheus, the mortal who stole fire from the gods, and how Zeus exacted revenge on humankind. Zeus ordered Hephaestus to fashion a beautiful woman, animated by Athena and sent to Earth by Hermes. Named Pandora, she bears a jar of 'gifts': sickness, grief and all the ills of life. Opening the jar to set these plagues upon humanity, Pandora slams the lid before hope can escape. It is pictured by some as divine consolation; but that is wishful thinking. The jar brings curses, of which hope is one. As Hesiod explains: 'The dope / Who's idle and awaits an empty hope, / Gripes in his soul, lacking a livelihood. / But as provider, Hope is not much good.' We cross our fingers, hoping it will all work out, instead of taking arduous, uncertain steps to make that happen. For Hesiod, hope is a narcotic.

Although it seems to cast hope as a plague, however, Hesiod's myth turns out to be equivocal. The question is what it means for hope to be left behind, imprisoned in the jar. It was being released that set the other plagues upon us. If hope remains confined, wouldn't that mean we are free of its temptations? Or is our curse to live *without* hope – in which case hope is something good, but something we can't have? Why, then, was it in Pandora's jar of ills? Hope seems impossible to place.

Until recently, I didn't think much about hope, and when I did, I was suspicious. My chronic pain is here to stay. To hope otherwise is to be dishonest. And when there's something to be done, what matters is to do it, not whether one does it with hope or resignation. Hope isn't important to me. My therapist disagrees. She believes that its significance in my life shows up in my resistance to it. The problem is that I'm afraid to hope; and what I need is courage.

It's not just me. For many, hope blurs into wishful thinking. And the more we hope, the more we risk despair. Why put ourselves through it? At the same time, we cling to hope, a seeming source of light when times are dark.

I have come to think that none of us are wrong. Hope is and ought to be an object of ambivalence. Imprisoned in Pandora's jar, hope is both useless and essential.

WHAT IS HOPE, ANYWAY? Philosophers have spilled some ink on this in recent years and, amid dissent, a broad consensus has emerged. Hope has elements of both desire and belief. To hope for something is, in part, to wish for it, in part to see it as possible, though not inevitable. You don't hope for what you don't want. Nor do you hope for what is out of the question or what you're sure is bound to happen. What's more, to hope for something is to think it isn't wholly up to you. It doesn't make sense to hope for what you can simply bring about. Hope is a concession to what you cannot control.

Both sides of hope – desiring and believing – take substantive forms. Thus hope is more than idle longing: it involves emotional attachment. That's why Søren Kierkegaard would speak of 'passion' in defining hope as 'a passion for what is possible'. In the same way, it's not enough to have what we might call 'idle belief'. By that I mean it's not enough for hope that you regard something as possible: you have to treat that possibility as 'live'. You needn't be optimistic; the odds can be as low as you like. But you have to take the prospect seriously in practice: it's the sort of thing you might plan for, if only as a contingency. (If you wish the blood test had been wrong, and you know that's possible, in principle, but you discount that possibility, you're no longer hoping that the test was clear.) When you're attached to a possibility you've discounted, your attitude towards it is despair. When attachment fades, you are resigned.

It is much easier to say why despair is bad than why hope is good. We despair when things are hopeless, but we remain attached to them. 'The relationship is over; she is gone forever,' cries the jilted lover. The terminal patient weeps: 'There is no cure.' What they feel is grief or something like it. The pain of passion for a possibility that has died.

But that doesn't mean there's merit in hope. Sometimes impossibility is a fact. My mother's Alzheimer's is not going to get better, only worse, and it would be foolish to hope otherwise, however much I wish it weren't. Even where hope is rational, what is the good of it? I think of the US elections in 2016 and 2020, when I watched the returns with agonised hope. There was nothing to do but manage my anxiety and vehemently plead for the better result. Where is the value in that? Hope coexists with quiescence. If there's courage in hoping, it's the courage to face the fear of disappointment that hope creates. When things turn out badly, hope is more harrowing than despair.

So Hesiod has a point. Hope can be deceptive, docile, daunting. Why celebrate its role in life? In a book she wrote in the wake of the 2003 invasion of Iraq, the writer and activist Rebecca Solnit rose to hope's defence:

'Hope is not like a lottery ticket you can sit on the sofa and clutch, feeling lucky,' she wrote. Instead,

> hope should shove you out the door, because it will take everything you have to steer the future away from endless war, from the annihilation of the earth's treasures and the grinding down of the poor and marginal. Hope just means another world might be possible, not promised, not guaranteed. Hope calls for action; action is impossible without hope.

The problem is that hope *can* be like clutching a lottery ticket and it needn't shove you out the door: as I know too well, you can hope intently as you stretch out on the sofa watching the news. The call for action comes from somewhere else.

Solnit may be right that action is impossible without hope: you cannot strive for what you care about, when success is not assured, without hoping to succeed or at least make progress. This is where the myth of hope's value starts. Hope is a precondition of what matters: the pursuit of meaningful change. But that doesn't make hope worthy in itself. Consider Prometheus, forging iron in the flames. He could not fashion ploughs or swords without fierce heat, but the temperature of the metal, the smoke and sparks, are means to an end, at best. Hope is like the forging point of iron: the temperature at which it can be wrought. Hope is the point at which we can be moved to act. But it is not the source of heat that brings us to that point or the force that moves us forwards, the hammer blow with which we bend the world. Like hot iron, hope is dangerous: it can hurt us. And by itself, hope does nothing at all.

Activists who valorise hope often recognise these facts. Thus Patrisse Cullors, one of the founders of Black Lives Matter, is quoted by Solnit in a later edition of her book. The mission of Black Lives Matter, Cullors wrote, is to provide 'hope and inspiration for collective action to build collective power to achieve collective transformation, rooted in grief and rage but pointed towards vision and dreams'. The driving forces here are grief and rage, not hope. Hope doesn't inspire us to act: it makes room for grief and rage to do that. Fear, too, can be a motivating force, as it is for those who work on climate change. 'I don't want you to be hopeful,' the activist Greta Thunberg told an audience at the World Economic Forum in Davos. 'I want you to panic.' Hope is consistent with inaction. It's a precondition of something good – of striving, uncertainly, for what matters – but it's not good in itself.

If you are trying to find a therapy for your illness, to adapt to disability, to cope with loneliness or escape from it, to succeed against the odds or to learn from failure, you are living in hope. Depending on your temperament, you may feel good about this or, like me, beset by fear. If hoping makes you anxious, you'll need courage. My therapist was right: I have to fight the fear of hope that inhibits me from taking risks. But hope itself is idle – a prerequisite, not a goal.

I SAID HOPE is and ought to be an object of ambivalence, but I've been mostly negative so far. Hope doesn't do much for us: at best it correlates with something good; and the correlation is imperfect. When we give up hope, we give up trying; but we can hope while doing nothing. And it's action, not hope, that matters.

The reason I'm ambivalent is that hope is not one thing. As well as the attitude one takes towards a given outcome when one hopes for it, there's the trait of being hopeful, finding hope where hope ought to be found. We can borrow here from the account of hope in the *Summa Theologica*, a three-thousand-page blockbuster of Catholic theology written by Saint Thomas Aquinas in the late thirteenth century. Aquinas contrasts hope as an 'irascible passion' – a spirited desire for what is not assured – with the theological virtue of hope whose object is eternal life. What we've examined is the passion: the fusion of desire and belief required for meaningful action. Hope in this sense can be passive, as the etymology of 'passion' attests. The theological virtue is different. It's an active propensity of the will through which one clings to the promise of union with God, fighting the temptations of despair. Although I am not religious – I don't believe in God, transcendence or immortality – I think we can discern a virtue on parallel lines.

Aquinas was inspired by Aristotle's theory of ethical virtue, on which a virtue is a 'mean' between opposing vices. Between recklessness and cowardice lies courage, for example; and the generous man is neither profligate nor cheap. Each virtue oversees an action or emotion for which it finds an intermediate path. The brave experience fear 'at the right times, with reference to the right objects, towards the right people, with the right motive, and in the right way'. Generosity is similar with giving and receiving.

Though Aristotle did not recognise hope as a virtue of character, his theory seems to fit. One can be excessively hopeful, inflating the odds or refusing to give up when possibilities are so distant they should vanish. Or one can be too hopeless, minimising chances or discounting risks that may be worth a shot. Virtue lies between these two extremes. To hope well is to be realistic about probabilities, not to succumb to wishful thinking or be cowed by fear; it is to hold possibilities open when you should. The point of clinging to possibility is not to feel good – hope may be more painful than despair – but to keep the flicker of potential agency alive.

I do not know if this is what Diogenes found precious, but it's a virtue one encounters in Solnit's book, the body of which is not a theory of hope but a history of the recent past, assembling evidence that change is possible, from the ending of apartheid in South Africa to the fall of the Berlin Wall, from the Zapatista uprising in Mexico to the legalising of same-sex marriage – then Occupy Wall Street, the Fossil Free movement and Black Lives Matter. Defying the 'angel of history' who surveys 'wreckage upon wreckage', unable to act, Solnit conjures 'the Angel of Alternate History' who tells us 'that our acts count, that we are making history all the time, because of what doesn't happen as well as what does . . . The Angel of History says, "Terrible," but this angel says, "Could be worse."' Resistance is not futile.

The virtue of hoping well is a matter of belief, of standing with or searching for the truth, attending to what's possible. And it's a matter of will, the courage to conceive alternatives, even when it's not clear what to do. This is how we should approach life's hardships, finding possibility where we can: the possibility of flourishing with disability or disease, of finding one's way through loneliness, failure, grief. The question, then, is not whether to hope but what we should hope for. In the spirit of this book, the answer's not an ideal life. What we need is acknowledgement and close reading of the lives we have. I can hope to ignore my pain or to make something of it, even if I don't hope for a cure. I can hope to see my mother again, to hold her hand and walk with her along the foreshore where the estuary gathers the tides and the great bridge sweeps across the river mouth, curving with the Earth. But I know she won't recover.

There are limits to hope, and death is one. Some dream of immortality by 'uploading', copying the contents of their mind to a machine. But as a simple argument shows, they are bound to fail – even if machines are some day conscious. Imagine you are uploaded but your brain is not erased, its 'data' preserved through the copying process. And suppose that the machine is brought online. There are two subjects now: you, as you were, and the machine. It is at best a mental duplicate of you, not you. But then the same is true if the machine is switched on when you die. You don't go on; you are merely copied.

There's no surviving death by natural means: it takes something transcendent, like reincarnation or the will of God. If you're not religious, you can't hope to live forever. Nor can you hope your loved ones will. It still makes sense to grieve their deaths: a form of rational despair. Each relationship is archived, each ability lost, one at a time or all at once but finally and forever. In the end, it seems, there is no hope: the lights go out.

But we have closed our eyes or cast them down. Look up and look around! There are billions of human beings and millions more are born each year. To paraphrase Franz Kafka, there is plenty of hope – no end of hope – only not for us. But that's too bleak. For who are we? Not just the living but humankind, and there is hope for humanity, and so for us. Again, the question is not whether to hope but what for. We can hope that life has meaning: a slow, unsteady march towards a more just future.

Nothing can right the wrongs of the past, which are with us forever, and the fight for a better world may be unending. But there is hope. Take climate change. Global warming cannot be averted. It has already happened and it is getting worse. But this disaster comes, quite literally, by degrees, and every increment makes a difference. When we cannot hope for two degrees, we can hope for two point five; when we cannot hope for that, we can hope for three. And in hoping, act together. We can hope that Earth will cool in time and with our efforts. Hope never dies: 'The worst is not / So long as we can say "This is the worst."'

When we do not know what we should hope for, we can hope to learn. It's hard to imagine, now, how to build a true democracy or what would count as meaningful reparation for the past. But there is space for what the philosopher Jonathan Lear calls 'radical hope . . . directed toward a future goodness that transcends the current ability to understand what it is'. With Iris Murdoch, we can hope that new concepts will 'extend . . . the limits of language, and enable it to illuminate regions which were formerly dark'.

Other concepts we should leave behind: the concept of the best life as a guideline or a goal, of being happy as the human good, of self-interest divorced from the good of others. Disability need not make life worse and pain is not lost for words. Love need not be earned; grief is no mistake; and the tempering of grief is not betrayal. Life is not a narrative 'that swells and tautens until climax'; it's not all about getting things done. Responsibility for justice need not rest on blame; and while we cannot know we've done enough, that's not a reason to do nothing. Human life is not inevitably absurd; there is room for hope.

Some of these discoveries are modern; some are new. But some have older roots. In 1991, the Irish poet Seamus Heaney wrote *The Cure at Troy*, adapting a play by the Greek playwright Sophocles first staged in 409 BCE, around the time Diogenes was born. The Greeks have besieged the city of Troy; Achilles, their hero, is dead; and they are told by a seer that the war cannot be won without Philoctetes and his bow. The catch is that Philoctetes was abandoned by Odysseus on the way to Troy, his foot snake-bitten, infected and stinking. 'I am the one / That dumped him,' Odysseus admits, 'him and his cankered foot – / Or what had been a foot before it rotted / And ate itself with ulcers.' The only hope is for Odysseus to return to the desert island Lemnos where Philoctetes waits. Odysseus brings with him Neoptolemus, Achilles's grieving son. The plan is for Neoptolemus to trick Philoctetes by painting Odysseus as their common foe, to bring Philoctetes back to Troy, and to win the war.

Things work out unexpectedly. Reluctant to lie, Neoptolemus initially goes ahead, earning Philoctetes's trust. But he is struck by shame when Philoctetes speaks: 'Imagine, son, / The bay all empty. The ships all disappeared. / Absolute loneliness. Nothing there except / The beat of the waves and the beat of my raw wound.' Neoptolemus confesses everything. And yet, he tells Philoctetes, the prophecy of the gods must be fulfilled. Philoctetes must come to Troy where Asclepius, the healer, will cure his wound. 'Then you're to take your bow and go with me / Into the front line and win the city. // All this must come to pass.' And so it does.

The Cure at Troy is a play about infirmity, loneliness, grief, failure, injustice, absurdity, hope. It's about the callousness with which we sometimes treat the sick and wounded, the loneliness of pain, the resilience of life in the teeth of suffering. It's about how grief can lead us into error, the vicissitudes of failure and success, the temptations of injustice and the prospect of repair. It's about the arc of the moral universe and the ways in which the mystery of the world, its unpredictability – the whim of the gods – creates or baffles meaning, how it makes space for hope, and for action. It's a plea for compassion, for courage, and a call for justice in an unjust world. Near the end of the play, the Chorus entreats Philoctetes to go to Troy and fight:

> History says, *Don't hope*
> *On this side of the grave.*
> But then, once in a lifetime
> The longed-for tidal wave
> Of justice can rise up,
> And hope and history rhyme.

The poet knows as well as we do that 'hope' and 'history' do not rhyme. But one day, in some undreamt-of harmony, they might.

Acknowledgements

My agent, Allison Devereux, made this book possible by telling me I didn't have to write it. I am grateful for her patience, tact and editorial wisdom. Most of all, I am grateful for her faith in me as a writer. Thank you, Allison.

Courtney Young at Riverhead was a generative, insightful editor. Her unerring eye for obscurity and muddy thinking saved me from many mistakes. Chris Wellbelove found the book a perfect home with Helen Conford at Hutchinson Heinemann. Thanks, Chris, and thank you, Helen, for reading with such care, for making my prose more eloquent and a little less judgemental, and for telling me what didn't work.

Several friends read drafts of this book in manuscript, to a deadline, in the summer of 2021. Thanks to Matt Boyle and Dick Moran for their engagement, encouragement and critique. They are, for me, two archetypes of intellectual integrity and I am grateful for their support. Ian Blecher sent me detailed comments on an earlier version of the book, inspiring numerous changes. I know I have not matched the brilliance of his own writing; but I have done my best. Thanks to Sara Nichols for emergency advice on the beginning of the book.

To Elle, and to Marah, I owe more than I can say. Their resilience and companionship keep me sane. From both of them, I have learned about love and loss, justice and failure. Elle is a beacon of poise, integrity and moral strength — but I would love them even if they weren't. Marah's genius influenced every chapter of this book. No one has done more to shape my intellectual life or my sense of what it means to be a writer. But then we have shaped each other's lives, inside and out, for twenty-five years. If we live in troubled times, I am lucky to be sharing them with her.

Notes

EPIGRAPH

vii 'You remind me': Quoted by his sister Hermine Wittgenstein in 'Mein Bruder Ludwig', *Ludwig Wittgenstein: Personal Recollections*, ed. Rush Rhees (Oxford, UK: Blackwell, 1981), 14–25, 18; thanks to Ian Blecher for help with the translation.

INTRODUCTION

1 we must say so: With apologies to John Berryman; see 'Dream Song 14', *The Dream Songs* (New York: Farrar, Straus and Giroux, 1969), 16: 'Life, friends, is boring. We must not say so.'

1 share of troubles: I trace my path to philosophy through the horror/sci-fi author H. P. Lovecraft in 'Correspondence: Revisiting H. P. Lovecraft', *Yale Review* 108: 135–52; published online as 'Lovecraft and Me', yale-review.org/article/lovecraft-and-me.

2 premature midlife crisis: I went on to write a book about it: *Midlife: A Philosophical Guide* (Princeton, NJ: Princeton University Press, 2017).

2 Inequality was rampant and democracy fragile: See Thomas Piketty, *Capital in the Twenty-First Century*, trans. Arthur Goldhammer (Cambridge, MA: Harvard University Press, 2014); Anne Applebaum, *Twilight of Democracy: The Seductive Lure of Authoritarianism* (New York: Doubleday, 2020).

2 'way we ought to live': Plato, *Republic*, trans. G. M. A. Grube and C. D. C. Reeve (1992), 352d, in Plato, *The Complete Works*, ed. John M. Cooper (Indianapolis: Hackett Publishing, 1997), 996.

3 philosophical ethics and 'self-help': See Aaron Garrett, 'Seventeenth-Century Moral Philosophy: Self-Help, Self-Knowledge, and the Devil's

Mountain', *Oxford Handbook of the History of Ethics*, ed. Roger Crisp (Oxford, UK: Oxford University Press, 2013), 229–79.

3 **choose any life at all:** See Gavin Lawrence, 'Aristotle and the Ideal Life', *Philosophical Review* 102 (1993): 1–34.

3 **'make ourselves immortal':** Aristotle, *Nicomachean Ethics*, trans. David Ross and ed. Lesley Brown (Oxford, UK: Oxford University Press, 2009), 1177b32–1178a2.

3 **good life, not the bad:** Among the exceptions is Alasdair MacIntyre (in *Dependent Rational Animals: Why Human Beings Need the Virtues* [Chicago: Open Court Publishing, 1999], 4): 'The question therefore arises: what difference to moral philosophy would it make, if we were to treat the facts of vulnerability and affliction and the related facts of dependence as central to the human condition?'

3 **'a life's going badly'; 'ill-being is largely neglected':** Shelly Kagan, 'An Introduction to Ill-Being', *Oxford Studies in Normative Ethics* 4 (2015): 261–88, 262, 263.

3 **'power of positive thinking':** This trend is criticised in two recent books: Barbara Ehrenreich, *Bright-Sided: How Positive Thinking Is Undermining America* (New York: Picador, 2009), and Oliver Burkeman, *The Antidote: Happiness for People Who Can't Stand Positive Thinking* (New York: Farrar, Straus and Giroux, 2012).

4 **entirely up to us:** See Epictetus, 'Handbook', *Discourses, Fragments, Handbook*, trans. Robin Hard (Oxford, UK: Oxford University Press, 2014); and for contemporary adaptations, William Irvine, *A Guide to the Good Life: The Ancient Art of Stoic Joy* (Oxford, UK: Oxford University Press, 2008) and Massimo Pigliucci, *How to Be a Stoic* (New York: Basic Books, 2017).

4 **theodicy has a life:** The philosopher Susan Neiman went so far as to rewrite the history of modern philosophy as a meditation on the facts of natural and moral evil; see *Evil in Modern Thought: An Alternative History of Philosophy* (Princeton, NJ: Princeton University Press, 2002).

5 **'man of perfect integrity'; 'from his scalp':** Stephen Mitchell, *The Book of Job* (San Francisco: North Point Press, 1987), 6, 8.

5 **'the truth about me'; 'fourteen thousand sheep':** Mitchell, *Book of Job*, 91.

6 **'I can only choose':** Iris Murdoch, *The Sovereignty of Good* (London: Routledge, 1970), 35–36.

6 **'no way out'**: Robert Frost, 'A Servant to Servants', *Complete Poems of Robert Frost* (New York: Holt, Rinehart and Winston, 1964), 83.

7 **simulates an ideal life:** The case of Maya is inspired by Robert Nozick's 'Experience Machine'; see *Anarchy, State, and Utopia* (Cambridge, MA: Harvard University Press, 1974), 42–45.

7 **'Humanity does *not*'**: Friedrich Nietzsche, *Twilight of the Idols* (1889), trans. Richard Polt (Indianapolis: Hackett Publishing, 1997), 6.

8 **'blinded with fire'**: Plato, *Republic*, 361e; Plato, *Complete Works*, 1002.

8 **end with 'the whole residual cosmos'**: William James, *The Varieties of Religious Experience: A Study in Human Nature* (1902), ed. Matthew Bradley (Oxford, UK: Oxford University Press, 2012), 35.

10 **'on this earth'**: John Berger, *Hold Everything Dear: Dispatches on Survival and Resistance* (New York: Vintage, 2007), 102.

10 **'reading' the world**: Simone Weil, 'Essay on the Concept of Reading' (1941/1946), *Late Philosophical Writings*, trans. Eric O. Springsted and Lawrence E. Schmidt (South Bend, IN: University of Notre Dame Press, 2015), 21–28.

11 **'Writing about moral philosophy'**: Bernard Williams, *Morality: An Introduction to Ethics* (Cambridge, MA: Cambridge University Press, 1972), xvii.

1. INFIRMITY

15 **a 'metaphorical penis'**: Sandra Gilbert and Susan Gubar, *The Madwoman in the Attic: The Woman Writer and the Nineteenth-Century Literary Imagination* (New Haven, CT: Yale University Press, 1979), 3.

15 **nod to Virginia Woolf**: Susan Gubar, *Memoir of a Debulked Woman: Enduring Ovarian Cancer* (New York: Norton, 2012); Virginia Woolf, 'On Being Ill', *The New Criterion* 4 (1926): 32–45.

15 **'She may as well'**: Hilary Mantel, 'Meeting the Devil', *London Review of Books*, November 4, 2010.

16 **'bed of pain'; 'aches and fatigue'**: Gubar, *Debulked Woman*, 143, 243.

17 **a category of malfunction:** See Christopher Boorse, 'On the Distinction between Disease and Illness', *Philosophy and Public Affairs* 5 (1977), 49–68, modified by Havi Carel, *Phenomenology of Illness* (Oxford, UK: Oxford University Press, 2016), 17.

17 'that of political minorities': Rosemarie Garland-Thomson, *Extraordinary Bodies: Figuring Physical Disability in American Literature and Culture* (New York: Columbia University Press, 1997), 6.

18 'a minority body': Elizabeth Barnes, *The Minority Body: A Theory of Disability* (Oxford, UK: Oxford University Press, 2016), 1. Like Barnes, I focus on the body: cognitive and psychological disability raise complications I cannot go into here. On this point, see Barnes, *Minority Body*, 3, and her 'Replies to Commentators', *Philosophy and Phenomenological Research* 100 (2020): 232–43.

18 'metaphysics' of disability: Garland-Thomson thinks of disability as the negative impact of 'impairment' (which is biological malfunction) in adverse social conditions (Garland-Thomson, *Extraordinary Bodies*, Chapters 1 and 2); Barnes thinks of it as the focus of the movement for disability rights (Barnes, *Minority Body*, Chapter 1).

18 paradigm of injury or harm: See Barnes, *Minority Body*, Chapters 2 and 3.

18 parable of the farmer's luck: Jon J Muth, *Zen Shorts* (New York: Scholastic, 2005).

19 'the enjoyment of life': Samuel R. Bagenstos and Margo Schlanger, 'Hedonic Damages, Hedonic Adaptation, and Disability', *Vanderbilt Law Review* 60 (2007): 745–800, 763. See also Daniel Gilbert, *Stumbling on Happiness* (New York: Vintage, 2006), 153; Erik Angner, Midge N. Ray, Kenneth G. Saag and Jeroan J. Allison, 'Health and Happiness among Older Adults', *Journal of Health Psychology* 14 (2009): 503–12; and Carel, *Phenomenology*, 131–35.

20 the best life is 'lacking in nothing': Aristotle, *Nicomachean Ethics*, trans. David Ross and ed. Lesley Brown (Oxford, UK: Oxford University Press, 2009), 1097b16.

20 'most desirable of things': Aristotle, *Nicomachean Ethics*, 1097b17.

20 'realize your potential': Jonathan Haidt, *The Happiness Hypothesis: Finding Modern Truth in Ancient Wisdom* (New York: Basic Books, 2006), 156–57.

21 incomparable short story: Herman Melville, *Bartleby the Scrivener* (Brooklyn: Melville House, 2004); originally published as 'Bartleby, the Scrivener: A Story of Wall-Street', *Putnam's Monthly Magazine*, November–December 1853.

21 'I would prefer not to': Melville, *Bartleby*, 17.

22 a good life is 'lacking in nothing': Aristotle, *Nicomachean Ethics*, 1097b16.

22 in 'communist society': Karl Marx and Friedrich Engels, *The German Ideology* (1846), in *Karl Marx: Selected Writings*, ed. David McLellan (Oxford, UK: Oxford University Press, 2000), 175–208, 185.

22 protecting and preserving: See Joseph Raz, *Value, Respect, and Attachment* (Cambridge, UK: Cambridge University Press, 2001).

23 Bill Veeck started life: The details in this paragraph are drawn from *Veeck as in Wreck: The Autobiography of Bill Veeck* (New York: Putnam, 1962), written by Bill Veeck with Ed Linn.

23 Surviving unexpectedly through: Harriet McBryde Johnson, *Too Late to Die Young* (New York: Picador, 2005), 15.

24 'too many variables': Johnson, *Too Late to Die Young*, 207–8.

24 on meaningful testimony: See Barnes, *Minority Body*, Chapter 4.

24 of moral education: See Mark Hopwood, '"Terrible Purity": Peter Singer, Harriet McBryde Johnson, and the Moral Significance of the Particular,' *Journal of the American Philosophical Association* 4 (2016): 637–55.

24 more short-lived than we expect: Bagenstos and Schlanger, 'Hedonic Damages, Hedonic Adaptation, and Disability'.

24 Sceptical philosophers will ask: See, for instance, Guy Kahane and Julian Savulescu, 'Disability and Mere Difference', *Ethics* 126 (2016): 774–88.

24 adapting to disability is hard: Barnes, *Minority Body*, 148.

24 someone's bodily autonomy: Barnes, *Minority Body*, 147.

24 mordant thought experiment: Seana Shiffrin, 'Wrongful Life, Procreative Responsibility, and the Significance of Harm', *Legal Theory* 5 (1999): 117–48, 127–28.

25 By the same token: Here I disagree with Barnes, who takes a more radical line: 'In fact, there is no discrepancy between the cases of causing an infant to be disabled and causing an infant to be non-disabled' (Barnes, *Minority Body*, 154).

26 'Objective measures [of health]': Erik Angner et al., 'Health and Happiness among Older Adults', 510.

28 'the shiver and the headache': Woolf, 'On Being Ill', 34.

28 'Physical pain – unlike': Elaine Scarry, *The Body in Pain: The Making and Unmaking of the World* (Oxford, UK: Oxford University Press, 1985), 5.

28 'has no referential content': See George Pitcher, 'Pain Perception', *Philosophical Review* 79 (1970): 368–93.

29 'Then what of': Mantel, 'Meeting the Devil'.

29 'or pathological state': Pitcher, 'Pain Perception', 371.

30 'No longer simply': Drew Leder, *The Absent Body* (Chicago: University of Chicago Press, 1990), 74. Leder is indebted to earlier phenomenologists, perhaps especially to Sartre on 'The Body'; see Jean-Paul Sartre, *Being and Nothingness* (1943), trans. Sarah Richmond (London: Routledge, 2018).

31 'Nature . . . teaches me': René Descartes, *Meditations on First Philosophy* (1641), trans. John Cottingham (Cambridge, UK: Cambridge University Press, 1986), 64.

31 'For us the body': Maurice Merleau-Ponty, *The Primacy of Perception: And Other Essays*, ed. James M. Edie (Evanston, IL: Northwestern University Press, 1964), 5, quoted in Carel, *Phenomenology*, 34.

32 called an 'electro-fink': David K. Lewis, 'Finkish Dispositions', *Philosophical Quarterly* 47 (1997): 143–58; C. B. Martin, 'Dispositions and Conditionals,' *Philosophical Quarterly* 44 (1994): 1–8.

32 'The prisoner imagines freedom': Alphonse Daudet, *In the Land of Pain* (1930), trans./ed. Julian Barnes (New York: Vintage, 2003), 44.

33 One of the key ideas of recent moral theory is 'the separateness of persons': The slogan is often attributed to John Rawls, but he doesn't use these words. He cites 'the distinction between persons' and 'the plurality and distinctness of individuals' (*A Theory of Justice* [Cambridge, MA: Harvard University Press, 1971], 27, 29). The phrase seems to derive, instead, from an obscure South African philosopher, J. N. Findlay, who parenthetically calls 'the separateness of persons . . . *the* basic facts for morals' (*Values and Intentions: A Study in Value-Theory and Philosophy of Mind* [London: Allen & Unwin, 1961], 299). See also Robert Nozick on 'side-constraints', or rights against interference, and 'the fact of our separate existences' (*Anarchy, State, and Utopia* [Cambridge, MA: Harvard University Press, 1974], 32–33).

34 'Strange aches; great flames': Daudet, *In the Land of Pain*, 6, 24–25.

36 'With chronic suffering': Leder, *Absent Body*, 76.

36 'Pain – has an Element of Blank': Emily Dickinson, *The Complete Poems* (New York: Little, Brown and Company, 1960), 323–24.

37 'Daudet's advice to': Daudet, *In the Land of Pain*, 79.

37 'piss for another man': The origin of the saying is a mystery. My research on pissing for others has turned up just one source: the Scottish philosopher and revolutionary John Oswald, who compared representative democracy

to the idea that we should 'piss by proxy', which is madness. See John Oswald, *The Government of the People, Or a Sketch of a Constitution for the Universal Commonwealth* (1792), quoted in David V. Erdman, *Commerce Des Lumières: John Oswald and the British in Paris, 1790–1793* (Columbia, MO: University of Missouri Press, 1986), 293.

38 'any oneness can hurt, too'; 'shared vistas of the terribly felt': Anne Boyer, *The Undying* (New York: Picador, 2019), 239.

39 'Painful hours spent': Daudet, *In the Land of Pain*, 25.

39 'natural way in': Carel, *Phenomenology*, 77.

2. LONELINESS

41 chronic loneliness, which persists: Emily White, *Lonely: Learning to Live with Solitude* (New York: Harper, 2010), 74–75.

42 2.5 billion people: Noreena Hertz, *The Lonely Century* (London: Sceptre, 2020), 1.

42 a podcast, *Five Questions*: Kieran Setiya, *Five Questions*, podcast audio, anchor.fm/kieran-setiya.

42 admonitory books about: David Riesman, Nathan Glazer and Reuel Denney, *The Lonely Crowd* (New Haven, CT: Yale University Press, 1950); Philip Slater, *The Pursuit of Loneliness* (Boston: Beacon Press, 1970); Vance Packard, *A Nation of Strangers* (Philadelphia: D. McKay Company, 1972); Robert D. Putnam, *Bowling Alone* (New York: Simon & Schuster, 2000); Sherry Turkle, *Alone Together* (New York: Basic Books, 2011).

42 about 'important matters': Miller McPherson, Lynn Smith-Lovin and Matthew E. Brashears, 'Social Isolation in America: Changes in Core Discussion Networks over Two Decades', *American Sociological Review* 71 (2006): 353–75; cited in John Cacioppo and William Patrick, *Loneliness: Human Nature and the Need for Social Connection* (New York: Norton, 2008), 52, 247; White, *Lonely*, 222–23; and Hertz, *The Lonely Century*, 10–11.

42 ideology of 'possessive individualism': C. B. Macpherson, *The Political Theory of Possessive Individualism: Hobbes to Locke* (Oxford, UK: Oxford University Press, 1962).

43 we get is 'oneliness': See Fay Bound Alberti, *A Biography of Loneliness* (Oxford, UK: Oxford University Press, 2019), 18–20.

43 not just the word: Alberti, *A Biography of Loneliness*, 10, 30–37.

43 "Tis strange with how little': Charles Dickens, *Sketches by Boz* (London: John Macrone, 1836), 'Thoughts about People'.

43 a 'statistical artifact': Claude S. Fischer, 'The 2004 GSS Finding of Shrunken Social Networks: An Artifact?' *American Sociological Review* 74 (2009): 657–69.

43 affecting the responses: Anthony Paik and Kenneth Sanchagrin, 'Social Isolation in America: An Artifact', *American Sociological Review* 78 (2013): 339–60.

43 wealth of evidence: Claude S. Fischer, *Still Connected: Family and Friends in America Since 1970* (New York: Russell Sage Foundation, 2011).

44 'without friends no one': Aristotle, *Nicomachean Ethics*, trans. David Ross and ed. Lesley Brown (Oxford, UK: Oxford University Press, 2009), 1155a5–6.

44 'A perfect solitude': David Hume, *A Treatise of Human Nature* (1739–40), eds. David Fate Norton and Mary J. Norton (Oxford, UK: Oxford University Press, 2007), 2.2.5.

44 'that inward eye': William Wordsworth, '"I Wandered Lonely as a Cloud"' (1804), *Selected Poems*, ed. Stephen Gill (London: Penguin, 2004), 164.

44 'love your solitude': Rainer Maria Rilke, *Letters to a Young Poet* (1929), trans. M. D. Herter Norton (New York: Norton, 1934), 30.

44 'Santa Claus of loneliness': W. H. Auden, 'New Year Letter', *Collected Poems* (New York: Vintage, 1976), 204.

44 generative power of being alone: Anthony Storr, *Solitude: A Return to the Self* (New York: Free Press, 1988).

45 early modern England: Keith Thomas, *The Ends of Life: Roads to Fulfilment in Early Modern England* (Oxford, UK: Oxford University Press, 2009), Chapter 6.

45 'In all these cases': Thomas, *The Ends of Life*, 191.

45 Scottish Enlightenment thinkers: Allan Silver, 'Friendship in Commercial Society: Eighteenth-Century Social Theory and Modern Sociology', *American Journal of Sociology* 6 (1990): 1474–504; Adam Smith, *An Inquiry into the Nature and Causes of the Wealth of Nations* (1776), eds. R. H. Campbell and A. S. Skinner (Oxford, UK: Oxford University Press, 1975).

45 less lonely, now: See David Vincent, *A History of Solitude* (Cambridge, UK: Polity, 2020), 153–55; Radclyffe Hall, *The Well of Loneliness* (London: Jonathan Cape, 1928).

45 social media damage: See Vincent, *A History of Solitude*, 251, responding to Turkle, *Alone Together*.

46 'Social isolation has an impact': Cacioppo and Patrick, *Loneliness*, 5.

46 not just 'comorbid' behaviours: Cacioppo and Patrick, *Loneliness*, 93–99.

46 associated with 'fight-or-flight': Cacioppo and Patrick, *Loneliness*, 105.

46 a nine-year study: L. F. Berkman and S. L. Syme, 'Social Networks, Host Resistance and Mortality: A Nine-Year Follow-up Study of Alameda County Residents', *American Journal of Epidemiology* 109 (1979): 186–204.

46 Functional MRIs show: Cacioppo and Patrick, *Loneliness*, 8.

47 the solitary self: 'I think, therefore I am': René Descartes, *Meditations on First Philosophy* (1641), ed. John Cottingham (Cambridge, UK: Cambridge University Press, 1986), 21.

47 no 'I' without 'you': See G. W. F. Hegel, *Phenomenology of Spirit* (1807), trans. A. V. Miller (Oxford, UK: Oxford University Press, 1977), and, more explicitly, the sections of the *Encyclopedia of the Philosophical Sciences* (1830) published as *Philosophy of Mind*, trans. W. Wallace and A. V. Miller, revised with introduction and commentary by Michael Inwood (Oxford, UK: Oxford University Press, 1971/2007).

47 'When we say "I think"': Jean-Paul Sartre, *Existentialism Is a Humanism* (1945), trans. Carol Macomber (New Haven, CT: Yale University Press, 2007), 41.

47 no 'private language': Ludwig Wittgenstein, *Philosophical Investigations*, trans. G. E. M. Anscombe (Oxford, UK: Blackwell, 1953).

49 'man is by nature': Aristotle, *Politics*, trans. Ernest Barker and ed. R. F. Stalley (Oxford, UK: Oxford University Press, 1995), 1253a.

49 Our distinctive sociality; The story of human evolution: See Michael Tomasello, *A Natural History of Human Thinking* (Cambridge, MA: Harvard University Press, 2014).

49 Monkeys deprived of physical contact: Cacioppo and Patrick, *Loneliness*, 129–30.

49 among homeless children: Inge Bretherton, 'The Origins of Attachment Theory: John Bowlby and Mary Ainsworth', *Developmental Psychology* 28 (1992): 759–75, 760–2.

49 orphans raised en masse: Cacioppo and Patrick, *Loneliness*, 130–31.

50 'attachment styles' developed: Cacioppo and Patrick, *Loneliness*, 132–33.

50 'closed cells for twenty-two': Jean Casella and James Ridgeway, 'Introduction', *Hell Is a Very Small Place*, eds. Jean Casella, James Ridgeway, and Sarah Shourd (New York: New Press, 2016), 1–20, 7.

50 'submitted to complete isolation': Quoted in Casella and Ridgeway, 'Introduction', 3.

50 'The clinical impacts': Quoted in Casella and Ridgeway, 'Introduction', 10–11.

50 even used in schools: Dan Moshenberg, 'For Vulnerable Children, the School Day Can Include Solitary Confinement', *Solitary Watch*, January 30, 2020, solitarywatch.org/2020/01/30/for-vulnerable-children-the-school-day-can-include-solitary-confinement.

51 'the *unsociable sociability*'; 'lies in human nature': Immanuel Kant, 'Idea for a Universal History with a Cosmopolitan Aim' (1784), in *Anthropology, History, and Education*, eds. Robert B. Louden and Günter Zöller (Cambridge, UK: Cambridge University Press, 2007), 111.

51 famous for dinner parties: See Manfred Kuehn, *Kant: A Biography* (Cambridge, UK: Cambridge University Press, 2001), 322–25.

51 'The entirety of hell'; 'Hell is other people': Victor Hugo, *La Fin de Satan* (1886), trans. R. G. Skinner, in *God and the End of Satan: Selections* (Chicago: Swan Isle Press, 2014); Jean-Paul Sartre, *No Exit* (1944), trans. Stuart Gilbert, in *No Exit and Three Other Plays* (New York: Vintage, 1989).

51 'an almost infinite trial': Thomas Merton, 'Notes for a Philosophy of Solitude', *Disputed Questions* (New York: Farrar, Straus and Giroux, 1960), 190.

52 *philia*, which is commonly: Aristotle, *Nicomachean Ethics*, Books VIII and IX.

54 'only what is good': Aristotle, *Nicomachean Ethics*, 1165b13–14.

55 known as 'epistemic partiality': Simon Keller, 'Friendship and Belief', *Philosophical Papers* 33 (2004): 329–51; Sarah Stroud, 'Epistemic Partiality in Friendship,' *Ethics* 116 (2006): 498–524.

55 'Concern for the friendship': Michael Stocker, 'Values and Purposes: The Limits of Teleology and the Ends of Friendship', *Journal of Philosophy* 78 (1981): 747–65, 755.

56 'What has a price': Immanuel Kant, *Groundwork of the Metaphysics of Morals* (1785), trans. Mary Gregor (Cambridge, UK: Cambridge University Press, 1998), 46–47.

56 That is why the philosopher: J. David Velleman, 'Love as a Moral Emotion', *Ethics* 109 (1999): 338–74; see also Kieran Setiya, 'Love and the Value of a Life', *Philosophical Review* 123 (2014): 251–80.

56 a 'required minimum'; 'optional' but apt: Velleman, 'Love as a Moral Emotion', 366.

57 Imprisoned for drug offences: Five Mualimm-ak, 'Invisible', *Hell Is a Very Small Place*, 147–52, 147.

57 'The very essence': Mualimm-ak, 'Invisible', 149.

57 the key of Kafka: Haruki Murakami, *Colorless Tsukuru Tazaki and His Years of Pilgrimage* (New York: Vintage, 2014).

58 'It was as if': Murakami, *Colorless Tsukuru Tazaki*, 4.

58 'The reason why': Murakami, *Colorless Tsukuru Tazaki*, 5.

58 'Think about it': Murakami, *Colorless Tsukuru Tazaki*, 32.

58 'things I need': Murakami, *Colorless Tsukuru Tazaki*, 194.

59 'still something stuck': Murakami, *Colorless Tsukuru Tazaki*, 193.

59 'I'd tell myself': White, *Lonely*, 162.

59 attentive to social cues: Cacioppo and Patrick, *Loneliness*, 161; the rest of this paragraph draws on Chapter 10.

59 lack of social skills: White, *Lonely*, 148–49.

60 'Dutch psychologist Nan Stevens': White, *Lonely*, 274–75.

60 'The most difficult': Cacioppo and Patrick, *Loneliness*, 230–31.

61 to 'start small': Cacioppo and Patrick, *Loneliness*, 237.

61 a soup kitchen; women's basketball league: White, *Lonely*, 67.

61 'was able to offset': White, *Lonely*, 309.

62 study of commuters: Nicholas Epley and Juliana Schroeder, 'Mistakenly Seeking Solitude', *Journal of Experimental Psychology* 143 (2014): 1980–99, cited in Kate Murphy, *You're Not Listening: What You're Missing and Why It Matters* (New York: Celadon Books, 2020), 42–46.

62 growing up with strabismus: Stephen Darwall, interviewed by Kieran Setiya, *Five Questions*, May 18, 2021, anchor.fm/kieran-setiya/episodes /Stephen-Darwall-es59ce.

62 heart of ethics: Stephen Darwall, *The Second-Person Standpoint: Morality, Respect, and Accountability* (Cambridge, MA: Harvard University Press, 2006).

62 learning how to listen well: For a recent overview, see Murphy, *You're Not Listening*.

63 'We realize too little': F. P. Ramsey, 'Epilogue', *Philosophical Papers*, ed. D. H. Mellor (Cambridge, UK: Cambridge University Press, 1990), 245–50, 247.

63 shown how structured conversation: Murphy, *You're Not Listening*, 150–51, 179–80.

3. GRIEF

65 'My mother just died': Tig Notaro, 'No Questionnaires to Dead People', *Live* (Secretly Canadian, 2012).

66 not a simple emotion: See George A. Bonanno, *The Other Side of Sadness: What the New Science of Bereavement Tells Us about Life After Loss* (New York: Basic Books, 2009), 34.

66 'I am suffering': Roland Barthes, *Mourning Diary: October 26, 1977– September 15, 1979* (2009), trans. Richard Howard (New York: Hill & Wang, 2010), 122.

66 And then there are those: On the prevalence of laughter in bereavement, see Bonanno, *Other Side of Sadness*, 38–39.

66 something we *do*: On the dynamic character of grief, see Peter Goldie, 'Grief: A Narrative Account', *Ratio* 24 (2011): 119–37. As will emerge, however, I don't think it's helpful to conceive the temporality of grief as that of beginning, middle and end.

66 'Grief turns out': Joan Didion, *The Year of Magical Thinking* (New York: Vintage, 2005), 188–89.

67 'complicated grief reactions': Bonanno, *Other Side of Sadness*, 103.

68 Freudian notion of 'grief work': Bonanno, *Other Side of Sadness*, 15–20.

68 being forced to 'debrief': Bonanno, *Other Side of Sadness*, 107–8.

68 in predictable stages: Bonanno, *Other Side of Sadness*, 21–22. The five-stage model copies Kübler-Ross on the process by which the terminally ill confront their own mortality; see Elisabeth Kübler-Ross, *On Death & Dying* (New York: Scribner, 1969).

68 'Bereavement is essentially': Bonanno, *Other Side of Sadness*, 40.

68 quartered sheets of typing paper: Barthes, *Mourning Diary*, ix.

68 'hastily, in the turmoil': Annie Ernaux, *I Remain in Darkness* (1997), trans. Tanya Leslie (New York: Seven Stories Press, 1999), 10.

69 a book in a box: B. S. Johnson, *The Unfortunates* (London: Panther Books, 1969).

69 ancient Greece and Rome: For an overview, see Scott LaBarge, 'How (and Maybe Why) to Grieve Like an Ancient Philosopher', *Oxford Studies in Ancient Philosophy, Supplementary Volume* (2012): 321–42.

70 'With regard to everything': Epictetus, 'Handbook', *Discourses, Fragments, Handbook*, trans. Robin Hard (Oxford, UK: Oxford University Press, 2014), 288.

70 **popularity of Stoic thought:** For contemporary versions, see William Irvine, *A Guide to the Good Life: The Ancient Art of Stoic Joy* (Oxford, UK: Oxford University Press, 2008), and Massimo Pigliucci, *How to Be a Stoic* (New York: Basic Books, 2017).

71 **the novelist Henry James:** See Beth Blum, *The Self-Help Compulsion: Searching for Advice in Modern Literature* (New York: Columbia University Press, 2020), 225–26.

71 **to sour grapes:** See Jon Elster, *Sour Grapes: Studies in the Subversion of Rationality* (Cambridge, UK: Cambridge University Press, 1983).

71 **to accommodate oppression:** See Martha Nussbaum, 'Adaptive Preferences and Women's Options', *Economics and Philosophy* 17 (2001): 67–88.

71 **as divinely ordered:** John M. Cooper, *Pursuits of Wisdom: Six Ways of Life in Ancient Philosophy from Socrates to Plotinus* (Princeton, NJ: Princeton University Press, 2012), Chapter 4.

72 **it rests on a theodicy:** This fact is emphasised by Carlos Fraenkel in his critique of Pigliucci, 'Can Stoicism Make Us Happy?', *The Nation*, 5 February 2019.

72 **'Never pretend that the things':** A. O. Bell, ed., *The Diary of Virginia Woolf, Volume 2: 1920–1924* (New York: Harcourt Brace & Company, 1978), 221.

72 **'You die at':** Iris Murdoch, *The Sea, the Sea* (London: Chatto & Windus, 1978), 84.

73 **'someone we didn't know':** Stacey May Fowles, *Baseball Life Advice: Loving the Game That Saved Me* (Toronto, ON: McClelland & Stewart, 2017), 224.

73 **'Life changes fast':** Didion, *Magical Thinking*, 3.

74 **In 'completed' relationships; in 'archived' relationships:** Samuel Scheffler, 'Aging as a Normative Phenomenon', *Journal of the American Philosophical Association* 2 (2016): 505–22, 505–6.

75 **'This is what those'; 'I talk to her constantly':** Julian Barnes, 'The Loss of Depth', in *Levels of Life* (New York: Vintage, 2013), 111.

75 **'Whenever I need':** Denise Riley, 'Time Lived, Without Its Flow' (2012), in *Say Something Back; Time Lived, Without Its Flow* (New York: New York Review Books, 2020), 69–124, 98.

75 **out of engagement:** On this point, see Scheffler, 'Aging as a Normative Phenomenon', 514–18.

76 **'By what means':** Denise Riley, 'Time Lived, Without Its Flow', 100.

76 **can seem 'intolerably high'; 'The dead slip away':** Denise Riley, 'Time Lived, Without Its Flow', 121.

76 'It's your mother': Palle Yourgrau, *Death and Nonexistence* (Oxford, UK: Oxford University Press, 2019), 49.

77 'the next figure': C. S. Lewis, *A Grief Observed* (London: Faber and Faber, 1961), 50.

77 comfort in memories: Bonanno, *Other Side of Sadness*, 72–74.

77 'The more joy': Lewis, *A Grief Observed*, 54.

77 called 'Pure mourning': Barthes, *Mourning Diary*, 40.

77 the ancient schools agree: See, again, LaBarge, 'How (and Maybe Why) to Grieve Like an Ancient Philosopher'.

78 'So death, the most terrifying': Epicurus, 'Letter to Menoeceus', *Epicurus: The Extant Remains*, trans. Cyril Bailey (Oxford, UK: Oxford University Press, 1926), 82–93, 85.

78 'Her body, her spirit': Barnes, 'Loss of Depth', 85.

78 wanted to be Superman: Kieran Setiya, *Midlife: A Philosophical Guide* (Princeton, NJ: Princeton University Press, 2017), 118–19.

80 'This morning she got up': Ernaux, *I Remain in Darkness*, 19.

80 'It breaks my heart': Ernaux, *I Remain in Darkness*, 39.

81 'horror and helplessness': Ernaux, *I Remain in Darkness*, 70.

81 'overcome with grief': Ernaux, *I Remain in Darkness*, 71.

82 a partner or child are 'emotionally resilient': Bonanno, *Other Side of Sadness*, 6–8, 70, 96; George A. Bonanno, Judith Tedlie Moskowitz, Anthony Papa and Susan Folkman, 'Resilience to Loss in Bereaved Spouses, Bereaved Parents, and Bereaved Gay Men', *Journal of Personal and Social Psychology* 88 (2005): 827–43.

82 'Most bereaved people': Bonanno, *Other Side of Sadness*, 24.

82 'Does being able': Barthes, *Mourning Diary*, 68.

82 'I was surprised': Berislav Marušić, 'Do Reasons Expire? An Essay on Grief', *Philosophers' Imprint* 18 (2018): 1–21, 2–3. See also Dan Moller, 'Love and Death', *Journal of Philosophy* 104 (2007): 301–16.

83 The same thing goes for love: In thinking through love, I am indebted to Patrick Quinn White, *Love First*, (PhD thesis, MIT, 2019), dspace.mit.edu /handle/1721.1/124091.

84 unintelligible from within: See Marušić, 'Do Reasons Expire?' 17–18, though he overstates the paradox by clinging to the equation of what makes sense with what we have reason to feel.

84 with social support: Bonanno, *Other Side of Sadness*, 75–76.

85 The Dahomey of Western Africa; The Saramaka in Surinam: Bonanno, *Other Side of Sadness*, 163–64.

85 of paper replicas: Bonanno, *Other Side of Sadness*, 171–74.

85 'parents and children': David Konstan, *The Emotions of the Ancient Greeks* (Toronto, ON: University of Toronto Press, 2006), 252.

85 no natural resolution: Konstan, *Emotions of the Ancient Greeks*, 247, 253.

85 For much of Western history: This paragraph draws on Philippe Ariès, *Western Attitudes toward Death: From the Middle Ages to the Present* (Baltimore, MD: Johns Hopkins University Press, 1974).

86 in World War I: Geoffrey Gorer, *Death, Grief, and Mourning in Contemporary Britain* (New York: Doubleday, 1965).

89 'Shall I keep': Lydia Davis, 'How Shall I Mourn Them?', *The Collected Stories of Lydia Davis* (New York: Picador, 2009), 697–99.

89 'What is "success"': Barnes, 'Loss of Depth', 125–26.

4. FAILURE

91 philosophically resonant and linguistically well served: Kieran Setiya, 'Going Deep: Baseball and Philosophy', *Public Books*, October 23, 2017, www.publicbooks.org/going-deep-baseball-and-philosophy.

92 'If we remembered': James Richardson, *Vectors: Aphorisms & Ten-Second Essays* (Keene, NY: Ausable Press, 2001), 91.

92 'who neither learnt': Joe Moran, *If You Should Fail: A Book of Solace* (London: Viking, 2020), 148–49.

93 great studies of social failure: Christopher Hill, *The Experience of Defeat* (London: Verso Books, 1984).

94 unwinds the knot: Joshua Prager, *The Echoing Green: The Untold Story of Bobby Thomson, Ralph Branca, and the Shot Heard Round the World* (New York: Vintage, 2006).

94 'Pitcher and hitter': Prager, *Echoing Green*, 215.

95 'Thus did a bloody': Prager, *Echoing Green*, 7, 11, 13.

95 'The foundational myth': Moran, *If You Should Fail*, 4.

96 most vocal critic: Galen Strawson, 'A Fallacy of Our Age', *Things That Bother Me: Death, Freedom, the Self, Etc.* (New York: New York Review

Books, 2018); the essay is a more accessible revision of Strawson's classic 'Against Narrativity', *Ratio* 17 (2004): 428–52.

96 **'Each of us constructs':** Oliver Sacks, *The Man Who Mistook His Wife for a Hat* (New York: Touchstone, 1985), 110.

96 **'We *become* the autobiographical':** Jerome Bruner, 'Life as Narrative', *Social Research* 54 (1987), 11–32, 15.

96 **philosophical big hitters:** Alasdair MacIntyre, *After Virtue* (South Bend, IN: Notre Dame University Press, 1981); Daniel Dennett, 'Why Everyone Is a Novelist', *Times Literary Supplement*, September 16, 1988; Charles Taylor, *The Sources of the Self* (Cambridge, MA: Harvard University Press, 1989); Paul Ricoeur, *Oneself as Another* (1990), trans. Kathleen Blamey (Chicago: University of Chicago Press, 1992).

96 **'an unfolding story':** Taylor, *Sources of the Self*, 47.

96 **'all virtuoso novelists':** Dennett, 'Why Everyone Is a Novelist'.

96 **'I have absolutely':** G. Strawson, 'A Fallacy of Our Age', 51.

97 **Strawson senior is known:** See P. F. Strawson, 'Freedom and Resentment', *Proceedings of the British Academy* 48 (1962): 187–211; P. F. Strawson, *Individuals* (London: Routledge, 1959).

97 **Galen was precocious:** G. Strawson, 'Introduction', *Things That Bother Me*, 13.

97 **nicely verbed by Strawson:** G. Strawson, 'The Unstoried Life', *Things That Bother Me*, 178: 'I don't think everyone stories themselves, and I don't think it's always a good thing'.

98 **Strawson cites illustrious forebears:** G. Strawson, 'A Fallacy of Our Age', 50.

98 **we might add Bill Veeck:** See Bill Veeck, with Ed Linn, *Veeck as in Wreck: The Autobiography of Bill Veeck* (New York: Putnam, 1962).

98 **Consider Murdoch, who studied classics:** My account of Murdoch's biography is drawn from Peter J. Conradi, *Iris Murdoch: A Life* (New York: Norton, 2001).

98 **also her first:** Iris Murdoch, *Under the Net* (London: Chatto & Windus, 1954).

98 **'innumerable intentions and charms':** Iris Murdoch, 'Literature and Philosophy: A Conversation with Bryan Magee', in *Existentialists and Mystics: Writings on Philosophy and Literature*, ed. Peter J. Conradi (London: Chatto & Windus, 1997), 4.

99 **'an Agent, an Action':** Bruner, 'Life as Narrative', 18. Bruner is drawing on Kenneth Burke, *The Grammar of Motives* (New York: Prentice-Hall, 1945).

99 'For centuries there's been one'; 'something that swells'; 'Bit masculo-sexual, no': Jane Alison, *Meander, Spiral, Explode* (New York: Catapult, 2019), 6.

99 Stories meander, spiral: See Alison, *Meander, Spiral, Explode*, 21–23.

99 journey on an escalator: Nicholson Baker, *The Mezzanine* (New York: Grove Press, 1988).

100 path to self-understanding: For this argument, see Helena de Bres, 'Narrative and Meaning in Life', *Journal of Moral Philosophy* 15 (2018): 545–71, though she acknowledges other means to intelligibility. See also Rahel Jaeggi, *Alienation*, trans. Frederick Neuhouser and Alan E. Smith, ed. Frederick Neuhouser (New York: Columbia University Press, 2014), on our continual need to 'appropriate' or take ownership of who we are.

100 'To call any life': Moran, *If You Should Fail*, 146.

101 'Observe, in short': Baker, *Mezzanine*, 120.

101 the digressive amplitude: For more on this, see Kieran Setiya, *Midlife: A Philosophical Guide* (Princeton, NJ: Princeton University Press, 2017), Chapters 3 and 4.

101 I had a midlife crisis: See, especially, Setiya, *Midlife*, Chapter 6.

102 problem of 'living in the present': Kieran Setiya, 'The Problem of "Living in the Present"', *New York Times*, September 11, 2017.

103 'frustration be the same': Bhagavad Gita, trans. Laurie L. Patton (London: Penguin, 2008), 29.

103 *The Idiot*'s composition: See Gary Saul Morson, 'Return to Process: The Unfolding of *The Idiot*', *New Literary History* 40 (2009): 843–65, 856; the rest of the paragraph draws on this wonderful essay.

103 *'a perfectly beautiful man'*: Dostoevsky quoted in Joseph Frank, *Dostoevsky: The Miraculous Years, 1865–1871* (Princeton, NJ: Princeton University Press, 1995), 271.

104 'Two weeks went by': Fyodor Dostoevsky, *The Idiot* (1869), trans. Richard Pevear and Larissa Volokhonsky (New York: Vintage, 2001), 572–73.

104 no guiding structure: See Morson, 'Return to Process', 854.

105 'Oh, you may': Dostoevsky, *The Idiot*, 394.

105 *'Happiness lies not'*: Fyodor Dostoevsky, *A Writer's Diary: Volume One, 1873–1876*, trans. Kenneth Lantz (Evanston, IL: Northwestern University Press, 1993), 335.

106 since 'if you are learning'; 'that sort of action': Aristotle, *Metaphysics* (9.6,

1048b18–34), as translated in Aryeh Kosman, *The Activity of Being* (Cambridge, MA: Harvard University Press, 2013), 40.

106 **jargon from linguistics:** Bernard Comrie, *Aspect* (Cambridge, UK: Cambridge University Press, 1976), §2.2.

107 **That is what the Bhagavad Gita:** Bhagavad Gita, 29.

108 **'But if you are':** Aristotle, *Metaphysics* (9.6, 1048b18–34), as translated in Kosman, *Activity of Being*, 40.

109 **'And here I end':** Quoted in John Gurney, *Gerrard Winstanley: The Digger's Life and Legacy* (London: Pluto Press, 2012), 73.

109 **'exhausted and bitterly disillusioned':** Hill, *Experience of Defeat*, 39.

109 **in a folk song:** Leon Rosselson, 'The World Turned Upside Down', *That's Not the Way It's Got to Be*, with Roy Bailey (Fuse Records, 1975).

109 **the anchor of my soundtrack:** Billy Bragg, 'The World Turned Upside Down', *Between the Wars* EP (Go! Records, 1985).

110 **Danny Rubin masterpiece:** *Groundhog Day* (Columbia Pictures, 1993), directed by Harold Ramis, screenplay by Danny Rubin and Harold Ramis.

111 **most careful estimate:** For details, see Simon Gallagher, 'Just How Many Days Does Bill Murray REALLY Spend Stuck Reliving Groundhog Day', *WhatCulture*, February 2, 2011, whatculture.com/film/just-how-many-days-does-bill-murray-really-spend-stuck-reliving-groundhog-day.

111 **by Buddhist philosophy:** My account of Buddhism draws on the work of Donald S. Lopez, Jr.: *The Story of Buddhism: A Concise Guide to Its History and Teachings* (New York: HarperCollins, 2001) and *The Scientific Buddha: His Short and Happy Life* (New Haven, CT: Yale University Press, 2012).

112 **meditation as a way:** See Setiya, *Midlife*, 145–54. This differs sharply from Buddhist meditation to the insight of *anattā* or 'no-self'.

112 **noun for people:** Scott A. Sandage, *Born Losers: A History of Failure in America* (Cambridge, MA: Harvard University Press, 2005), 11–12. See also Moran, *If You Should Fail*, 26.

113 **'More than a bank':** Sandage, *Born Losers*, 103, 134.

113 **'There is always':** Quoted in Sandage, *Born Losers*, 74.

113 **'Gospel of Wealth':** Sandage, *Born Losers*, 249.

113 **most popular lecture:** Sandage, *Born Losers*, 222.

113 **'I do not think much'; 'When we find':** Frederick Douglass, 'Self-Made Men' (1859), *The Speeches of Frederick Douglass* (New Haven, CT: Yale University Press, 2018), 424–25, 426.

114 'only ordinary ability': Douglass, 'Self-Made Men', 428–29.

114 'The land stinks': Quoted in Sandage, *Born Losers*, 6.

114 'deaths of despair': Anne Case and Angus Deaton, *Deaths of Despair and the Future of Capitalism* (Princeton, NJ: Princeton University Press, 2020).

115 'I came to see the streets': Ta-Nehisi Coates, *Between the World and Me* (New York: One World, 2015), 33.

115 waste of mass incarceration: Michelle Alexander, *The New Jim Crow: Mass Incarceration in the Age of Colourblindness* (New York: New Press, 2010).

115 Employment is increasingly polarised: See Arne L. Kalleberg, *Good Jobs, Bad Jobs: The Rise of Polarized and Precarious Employment Systems in the United States, 1970s to 2000s* (New York: Russell Sage Foundation, 2011), cited by Malcolm Harris in *Kids These Days: Human Capital and the Making of Millennials* (New York: Little, Brown, 2017), 67–68, 72–73.

115 inequality has soared: See Harris, *Kids These Days*, 20–24, 40–41, 75, 86.

116 'human capital' seems: Again, see Harris, *Kids These Days*, 97–101.

116 possessive individualism that portrays: C. B. Macpherson, *The Political Theory of Possessive Individualism: Hobbes to Locke* (Oxford, UK: Oxford University Press, 1962).

116 the 'work ethic,' how avarice; with social solidarity: See Max Weber, *The Protestant Ethic and the Spirit of Capitalism* (1905), trans. Talcott Parsons (London: Routledge, 1930); David Wootton, *Power, Pleasure, and Profit: Insatiable Appetites from Machiavelli to Madison* (Cambridge, MA: Harvard University Press, 2018); and Waheed Hussain, 'Pitting People Against Each Other', *Philosophy and Public Affairs* 48 (2020): 79–113.

117 'Properly speaking, there are': Douglass, 'Self-Made Men', 419.

5. INJUSTICE

120 'is deeply ailing': Theodor Adorno, *Minima Moralia: Reflections from Damaged Life* (1951), trans. E. F. N. Jephcott (London: Verso Books, 1974), §128.

120 'When he realized': Plato, *Republic*, trans. G. M. A. Grube and C. D. C. Reeve (1992), 359d–60a; in Plato, *Complete Works*, ed. John M. Cooper (Indianapolis: Hackett Publishing, 1997), 1000.

120 'Now, no one': Plato, *Republic*, 360bc; Plato, *Complete Works*, 1001.

121 is Glaucon's cynicism: According to evidence compiled by the evolutionary anthropologist Michael Tomasello, 'Most contemporary human beings,

if given [a ring] which would make their actions invisible to others, would still behave morally most of the time' (*A Natural History of Human Morality* [Cambridge, MA: Harvard University Press, 2016], 160).

121 'Philosophy is a battle'; 'The decisive movement': Ludwig Wittgenstein, *Philosophical Investigations*, trans. G. E. M. Anscombe (Oxford, UK: Blackwell, 1953), 47, 103.

123 the rations allowed: See Palle Yourgrau, *Simone Weil* (London: Reaktion Books, 2011), 97, 101.

123 'When she learned': Yourgrau, *Simone Weil*, 16–17.

123 harrowed her frail physique: See Yourgrau, *Simone Weil*, 18, 41, 43, 50–54, 86–87.

123 'was often too tired': Yourgrau, *Simone Weil*, 86–87.

123 'What a beautiful room': Yourgrau, *Simone Weil*, 104.

124 Weil writes, 'Alexander's well-being': Yourgrau, *Simone Weil*, 35.

124 'Categorical Imperative in skirts': Yourgrau, *Simone Weil*, 26.

124 'The project may appear': Simone Weil, *Seventy Letters: Some Hitherto Untranslated Texts from Published and Unpublished Sources*, trans. Richard Rees (Oxford, UK: Oxford University Press, 1965), 146, letter to Maurice Schumann, July 30, 1942.

124 profound experiences of Christ: Yourgrau, *Simone Weil*, 64, 68.

124 'We do not know for': Simone Weil, *Letter to a Priest*, trans. A. F. Wills (London: Routledge, 1953), 8.

124 education of railroad workers: Yourgrau, *Simone Weil*, 39.

124 marches and strikes; criticised Leon Trotsky: Yourgrau, *Simone Weil*, 46, 49.

125 Spanish Civil War: Yourgrau, *Simone Weil*, 57.

125 the role of violence: Yourgrau, *Simone Weil*, 50.

125 'To clarify thought': Simone Weil, 'The Power of Words' (1937), in Simone Weil, *An Anthology*, ed. Siân Miles (London: Penguin, 2005), 228–58, 242.

125 we cannot be truly free: Immanuel Kant, *Groundwork of the Metaphysics of Morals* (1785), trans. Mary Gregor (Cambridge, UK: Cambridge University Press, 1998).

126 'A man who is tempted': Simone Weil, 'Essay on the Concept of Reading', (1941/1946), *Late Philosophical Writings*, trans. Eric O. Springsted and Lawrence E. Schmidt (South Bend, IN: University of Notre Dame Press, 2015), 21–28, 27.

126 'Thus at each': Weil, 'Essay on the Concept of Reading', 22–23.

127 **Think back to Bartleby:** Herman Melville, *Bartleby the Scrivener* (Brooklyn: Melville House, 2004), originally published as 'Bartleby, the Scrivener: A Story of Wall-Street', *Putnam's Monthly Magazine*, November–December 1853.

127 **Interpreting 'Bartleby':** See Leo Marx, 'Melville's Parable of the Walls', *Sewanee Review* 61 (1953): 602–27; Robert D. Spector, 'Melville's "Bartleby" and the Absurd', *Nineteenth-Century Fiction* 16 (1961): 175–77; Kingsley Widmer, 'The Negative Affirmation: Melville's "Bartleby"', *Modern Fiction Studies* 8 (1962): 276–86; Christopher W. Sten, 'Bartleby the Transcendentalist: Melville's Dead Letter to Emerson', *Modern Language Quarterly* 35 (1974): 30–44; Louise K. Barnett, 'Bartleby as Alienated Worker', *Studies in Short Fiction* 11 (1974): 379–85; Egbert S. Oliver, 'A Second Look at "Bartleby"', *College English* 6 (1944–45): 431–39; Frederick Busch, 'Thoreau and Melville as Cellmates', *Modern Fiction Studies* 23 (1977): 239–42; Michael Rogin, *Subversive Genealogy: The Politics and Art of Herman Melville* (New York: Knopf, 1985), 195.

127 **'human Xerox machines':** Andrew Delbanco, *Melville: His World and Work* (New York: Knopf, 2005), 214.

127 **'does him great violence':** Dan McCall, *The Silence of Bartleby* (Ithaca, NY: Cornell University Press, 1989), 98.

127 **'I can see that figure':** Melville, *Bartleby*, 15.

128 **'impotent rebellion . . . mild effrontery':** Melville, *Bartleby*, 29, 30, 33.

128 **is 'singularly sedate':** Melville, *Bartleby*, 15, 17.

128 **'pert and familiar'; 'D is discovered':** Iris Murdoch, *The Sovereignty of Good* (London: Routledge, 1970), 16–17.

128 **'impersonal quasi-scientific knowledge':** Murdoch, *Sovereignty*, 37.

129 **'The more the separateness':** Murdoch, *Sovereignty*, 64.

129 **'Altruists see the world differently':** Kristen Monroe, *The Heart of Altruism: Perceptions of a Common Humanity* (Princeton, NJ: Princeton University Press, 1996), 212.

129 **'Thought flies from affliction':** Simone Weil, *Waiting for God*, trans. Emma Craufurd (London: Routledge, 1951), 118.

130 **Love is, we found:** J. David Velleman, 'Love as a Moral Emotion', *Ethics* 109 (1999): 338–74. See also Kieran Setiya, 'Love and the Value of a Life', *Philosophical Review* 123 (2014): 251–80.

130 'Among human beings': Simone Weil, *Gravity and Grace* (1947), trans. Emma Craufurd and Mario von der Ruhr (London: Routledge, 1952), 64.

130 'Friendship has something universal': Weil, *Waiting for God*, 206.

130 'Love is the perception': Iris Murdoch, 'The Sublime and the Good' (1959), *Existentialists and Mystics: Writings on Philosophy and Literature*, ed. Peter J. Conradi (London: Chatto & Windus, 1997), 205–20, 215.

130 'the fat relentless ego': Murdoch, *Sovereignty*, 51.

131 'The task of moral philosophers': Iris Murdoch, 'Vision and Choice in Morality' (1956), *Existentialists and Mystics*, 76–98, 90.

131 work of John Rawls: See John Rawls, *A Theory of Justice* (Cambridge, MA: Harvard University Press, 1971).

131 For Rawls, political philosophy: My interpretation roughly follows A. John Simmons, 'Ideal and Nonideal Theory', *Philosophy and Public Affairs* 38 (2010): 5–36, and Ben Laurence, 'Constructivism, Strict Compliance, and Realistic Utopianism', *Philosophy and Phenomenological Research* 97 (2018): 433–53.

132 a 'realistic utopia': John Rawls, *The Law of Peoples, with 'The Idea of Public Reason Revisited'* (Cambridge, MA: Harvard University Press, 1999), 7, adapting Jean-Jacques Rousseau, *On the Social Contract* (1762), trans. Donald A. Cress (Indianapolis: Hackett Publishing, 1987).

132 strive for utopia: Simmons, 'Ideal and Nonideal Theory', 21–22.

132 America's past and present: See, for instance, David I. Roediger, *How Race Survived U.S. History: From Settlement and Slavery to the Obama Phenomenon* (London: Verso Books, 2008).

132 we can perceive injustice: On the limitations of ideal theory, see, among others, Amartya Sen, 'What Do We Want from a Theory of Justice', *Journal of Philosophy* 103 (2006): 215–38.

132 structures of oppression: Charles Mills, '"Ideal Theory" as Ideology', *Hypatia* 20 (2005): 165–84.

132 the 'Critical Theory': On the history of Critical Theory, see Stuart Jeffries, *Grand Hotel Abyss: The Lives of the Frankfurt School* (London: Verso Books, 2016).

133 impossible to know: Anthropological evidence is suggestive here, though inconclusive. See James Suzman, *Work: A Deep History, from the Stone Age to the Age of Robots* (New York: Penguin Press, 2021); an important precursor is Marshall Sahlins, *Stone Age Economics* (London: Routledge, 1974).

133 'an emancipated society'; 'fulfilment of human possibilities'; 'is tenderness only': Adorno, *Minima Moralia*, §100. In thinking through Adorno's view, I have been helped by Fabian Freyenhagen, *Adorno's Practical Philosophy: Living Less Wrongly* (Cambridge, UK: Cambridge University Press, 2013).

133 for 'effective altruism': See William MacAskill, *Doing Good Better: Effective Altruism and a Radical New Way to Make a Difference* (London: Faber and Faber, 2015), and Peter Singer, *The Most Good You Can Do: How Effective Altruism Is Changing Ideas about Living Ethically* (New Haven, CT: Yale University Press, 2015).

134 for neglecting politics: See Amia Srinivasan, 'Stop the Robot Apocalypse', *London Review of Books*, September 24, 2015.

134 a 'social connection model': Iris Marion Young, *Responsibility for Justice* (Oxford, UK: Oxford University Press, 2011).

135 'produce unjust outcomes': Young, *Responsibility for Justice*, 105.

135 in median wealth: Neil Bhutta, Andrew C. Chang, Lisa J. Dettling and Joanne W. Hsu, with assistance from Julia Hewitt, 'Disparities in Wealth by Race and Ethnicity in the 2019 Survey of Consumer Finances', 28 September 2020, www.federalreserve.gov/econres/notes/feds-notes/disparities-in-wealth-by-race-and-ethnicity-in-the-2019-survey-of-consumer-finances-20200928.htm.

135 Data on indigenous people: Jay L. Zagorsky, 'Native Americans' Wealth', in *Wealth Accumulation & Communities of Colour in the United States: Current Issues*, eds. Jessica Gordon Nembhard and Ngina Chiteji (Ann Arbor: University of Michigan Press, 2006), 133–54, 140.

135 'The almost insoluble': Adorno, *Minima Moralia*, §34.

136 'is not primarily'; 'Taking responsibility for': Young, *Responsibility for Justice*, 112.

136 'If I share responsibility': Young, *Responsibility for Justice*, 123.

136 Young confronts bystanders: Ben Laurence, 'The Question of the Agent of Change', *Journal of Political Philosophy* 28 (2020): 355–77.

137 At 2°C (3.6°F); Central Africa will lose; south and central Asia: Mark Lynas, *Our Final Warning: Six Degrees of Climate Emergency* (London: Fourth Estate, 2000), 76, 92–93, 96–97.

137 restrict our horizon to 1990; to current emissions: See Climate Watch, 'Historical GHG Emissions', www.climatewatchdata.org./ghg-emissions ?source=CAIT.

137 **Meanwhile, in sub-Saharan Africa:** Lynas, *Our Final Warning*, 91.

138 **class at MIT:** See David Chandler, 'Leaving Our Mark', MIT News, 16 April 2008, news.mit.edu/2008/footprint-tt0416.

138 **individual carbon footprint:** See Geoffrey Supran and Naomi Oreskes, 'Rhetoric and Frame Analysis of ExxonMobil's Climate Change Communications', *One Earth* 4 (2021): 696–719, 712.

138 **blue caution tape:** For details, see the press release from Fossil Free MIT: 'Four-Mile "Global Warming Flood Level" Demonstration Makes Waves Across MIT Campus', April 29, 2014, www.fossilfreemit.org/wp-content /uploads/2014/05/MIT-Press-Advisory-Fossil-Free-MIT-Climate -Change-Demonstration.pdf.

138 **Climate Change Conversation:** 'Report of the MIT Climate Change Conversation Committee: MIT and the Climate Challenge', June 2015, sustainability.mit.edu/sites/default/files/resources/2018-09/mit_climate _change_conversation_report_2015_0.pdf.

139 **first-ever Climate Action Plan:** 'A Plan for Action on Climate Change', October 21, 2015, web.mit.edu/climateaction/ClimateChangeStatement -2015Oct21.pdf.

139 **David Koch, perhaps:** 'David H. Koch, Prominent Supporter of Cancer Research at MIT, Dies at 79', MIT News, August 23, 2019, news.mit.edu /2019/david-koch-prominent-supporter-cancer-research-mit-dies-79-0823.

139 **a faculty protest; president's office, demanding more:** 'A Response to President Reif's Announced "Plan for Action on Climate Change"', 3 November 2015, web.mit.edu/fnl/volume/282/climate.html; Zahra Hirji, 'MIT Won't Divest, but Students End Protest After Compromise', 3 March 2016, insideclimatenews.org/news/03032016/mit-not-divest-students -sit-in-fossil-fuel-investment-climate-policy.

140 **'The philosophers have only':** Karl Marx, 'Theses on Feuerbach' (1845), in *Karl Marx: Selected Writings*, ed. David McLellan (Oxford, UK: Oxford University Press, 2000), 171–74, 173.

141 **'injustice and oppression':** Laurence, 'The Question of the Agent of Change', 376.

141 **Born in Frankfurt:** Stefan Müller-Doohm, *Adorno: A Biography* (2003), trans. Rodney Livingstone (Cambridge, UK: Polity, 2005), 13–16.

141 **Beethoven piano pieces; composition with Alban Berg:** Müller-Doohm, *Adorno*, 28, 98.

141 left for Oxford; polemic against jazz: Müller-Doohm, *Adorno*, 178, 199.

141 'Weimar on the Pacific': See Jeffries, *Grand Hotel Abyss*, 224.

142 'We are forgetting': Adorno, *Minima Moralia*, §21.

142 'What the philosophers': Adorno, *Minima Moralia*, Dedication.

142 contemporary György Lukács: György Lukács, *The Theory of the Novel* (1920), trans. Anna Bostock (Cambridge, MA: MIT Press, 1971), 22.

143 called the police; 'bared their breasts': Jeffries, *Grand Hotel Abyss*, 345, 347.

143 'He suggested that': Quoted in Jeffries, *Grand Hotel Abyss*, 321.

143 ten most wanted: See Jeffries, *Grand Hotel Abyss*, 321.

143 substitute for resistance: For a critique of Adorno on these lines, see Gillian Rose, *The Melancholy Science: An Introduction to the Thought of Theodor W. Adorno* (London: Verso Books, 1978), Chapter 7.

143 'wrong life cannot be lived': Adorno, *Minima Moralia*, §18.

144 those subjected to injustice: See Laurence, 'The Question of the Agent of Change', 371–73.

145 'right to your life': Richard Hugo, *The Triggering Town: Lectures and Essays on Poetry and Writing* (New York: Norton, 1979), 65.

146 called 'existential value': See Kieran Setiya, *Midlife: A Philosophical Guide* (Princeton, NJ: Princeton University Press, 2017), Chapter 2.

146 called 'the little human things': Zena Hitz, 'Why Intellectual Work Matters', *Modern Age* 61 (2017): 28–37.

146 'you've never gone hungry': The anecdote is recounted in Yourgrau, *Simone Weil*, 40.

6. ABSURDITY

147 Jean-Paul Sartre's 'nausea': Jean-Paul Sartre, *Nausea* (1938), trans. Lloyd Alexander (New York: New Directions, 2007).

147 'Never, until these'; 'Existence everywhere, infinitely': Sartre, *Nausea*, 127, 133.

148 'Why is there something': Gottfried Wilhelm Leibniz, 'Principles of Nature and of Grace, Based on Reason' (1714), *Philosophical Essays*, trans./ eds. Roger Ariew and Daniel Garber (Indianapolis: Hackett Publishing, 1989), 206–12, 210.

148 'If there were nothing': Quoted in Robert M. Martin, *There Are Two Errors*

in the the Title of This Book*: A Sourcebook of Philosophical Puzzles, Problems, and Paradoxes (Peterborough, ON: Broadview Press, 2012), 29.

148 **It's an impossible question:** For an entertaining exploration of attempts at an answer, see Jim Holt, *Why Does the World Exist?: An Existential Detective Story* (New York: Liveright Publishing, 2012).

150 **According to Wolf:** Susan Wolf, *Meaning in Life and Why It Matters* (Princeton, NJ: Princeton University Press, 2012).

150 **'My life came to':** Leo Tolstoy, 'A Confession' (1882), *A Confession and Other Religious Writings*, trans. Jane Kentish (London: Penguin, 1987), 17–80, 30.

151 **to find the Ultimate Question:** Douglas Adams, *The Ultimate Hitchhiker's Guide to the Galaxy* (New York: Del Rey, 2002).

152 **'If we learned that we'; 'Admittedly, the usual'; 'One is supposed':** Thomas Nagel, 'The Absurd', *Journal of Philosophy* 68 (1971): 716–27, 721.

152 **Remember Wittgenstein on:** Ludwig Wittgenstein, *Philosophical Investigations*, trans. G. E. M. Anscombe (Oxford, UK: Blackwell, 1953), 47.

153 **It appears in the mouth:** Thomas Carlyle, *Sartor Resartus* (1833–1834), ed. Kerry McSweeney and Peter Sabor (Oxford, UK: Oxford University Press, 1987), 140.

153 **'Thus in this':** Carlyle, *Sartor Resartus*, 57–58.

153 **'To me the Universe':** Carlyle, *Sartor Resartus*, 127.

154 **for early existentialists:** Søren Kierkegaard, *Either/Or: A Fragment of Life* (1843), trans. Alastair Hannay and ed. Victor Eremita (London: Penguin, 1992).

154 **attention, explanation, and affect:** This mode of interpretation stands in contrast to the 'hermeneutics of suspicion' or 'symptomatic reading' once dominant in literary studies; see Rita Felski, *The Limits of Critique* (Chicago: University of Chicago Press, 2015).

155 **'Religion, whatever it is'; 'sense of the whole residual cosmos':** William James, *The Varieties of Religious Experience* (1902), ed. Matthew Bradley (Oxford, UK: Oxford University Press, 2012), 35.

155 **'implies a religion':** Albert Einstein, *The World As I See It* (1934), trans. Alan Harris (London: Bodley Head, 1935), 1.

156 **'All Nature is':** Alexander Pope, *An Essay on Man* (1734), ed. Tom Jones (Princeton, NJ: Princeton University Press, 2018), 26–27.

157 **Modern philosophers detached:** Susan Neiman, *Evil in Modern Thought: An Alternative History of Philosophy* (Princeton, NJ: Princeton University Press, 2002).

157 **best of all possible:** Gottfried Wilhelm Leibniz, *Theodicy: Essays on the Goodness of God, the Freedom of Man, and the Origin of Evil* (1710), trans. E. M. Huggard (New Haven, CT: Yale University Press, 1952).

157 **Jean-Jacques Rousseau would:** See Neiman, *Evil in Modern Thought*, 37, 49–53.

157 **'insight to which':** G. W. F. Hegel, *Introduction to the Philosophy of History* (1837), trans. Leo Rauch (Indianapolis: Hackett Publishing, 1988), 39.

157 **'I accept the universe':** James, *Varieties of Religious Experience*, 39.

158 **'It is notorious':** James, *Varieties of Religious Experience*, 120.

158 **Ramsey was a prodigy:** He is the subject of a wonderful biography by Cheryl Misak, *Frank Ramsey: A Sheer Excess of Powers* (Oxford, UK: Oxford University Press, 2020).

158 **'Where I seem':** F. P. Ramsey, 'Epilogue', *Philosophical Papers*, ed. D. H. Mellor (Cambridge, UK: Cambridge University Press, 1990), 245–50, 249.

159 **'I don't feel':** Ramsey, 'Epilogue', 249–50.

159 **'silence of the world':** Albert Camus, *The Myth of Sisyphus* (1942), trans. Justin O'Brien (New York: Vintage, 1955), 28.

160 **humanity has become sterile:** P. D. James, *Children of Men* (New York: Vintage, 1992); *Children of Men*, cowritten and directed by Alfonso Cuarón (Universal Pictures, 2006).

160 **'those who lived'; 'It came upon us':** James, *Children of Men*, 9.

161 **'the cancellation of all'; 'the futility of all':** Jonathan Schell, *The Fate of the Earth* (New York: Knopf, 1982), 115, 169.

161 **to philosophical use:** Samuel Scheffler, *Death and the Afterlife*, ed. Niko Kolodny (Oxford, UK: Oxford University Press, 2013).

161 **'I find it plausible':** Scheffler, *Death and the Afterlife*, 40.

161 **a 'collective afterlife':** Scheffler, *Death and the Afterlife*, 64.

162 **'pleasure now comes':** James, *Children of Men*, 9; see Scheffler, *Death and the Afterlife*, 43.

163 **'the Alvy Singer problem':** Scheffler, *Death and the Afterlife*, 62–64, 188–90; *Annie Hall*, directed by Woody Allen (United Artists, 1977).

163 **voluntary human extinction:** Alan Weisman, *The World Without Us* (New York: St. Martin's Press, 2007), 241–44. For the record, I am sceptical of this view: there is no foundation for ethics outside of us, in Plato's Forms or Kant's Pure Reason; and an ethics based on us is bound to be anthropocentric. For a

sketch of what this means for parenthood, see Kieran Setiya, 'Creation: Pro(-) and Con', *Hedgehog Review* 23 (2021): 103–8.

164 **talk about 'ecological grief':** Ashlee Cunsolo and Neville R. Ellis, 'Ecological Grief as Mental Health Response to Climate Change-Related Loss', *Nature Climate Change* 8 (2018): 275–81.

164 **we have unfinished business:** For an expression of this idea in population ethics, see Jonathan Bennett, 'On Maximizing Happiness', *Obligations to Future Generations*, eds. R. I. Sikora and Brian Barry (Philadelphia: Temple University Press, 1978), 61–73.

166 **the pioneering theologian:** John Bowker, *The Meanings of Death* (Cambridge, UK: Cambridge University Press, 1991).

167 **For Hegel, history:** See G. W. F. Hegel, *Lectures on the Philosophy of World History* (1857), trans. H. B. Nisbet (Cambridge, UK: Cambridge University Press, 1975).

167 **'From each according to his ability':** Karl Marx, 'Critique of the Gotha Programme' (1875), in *Karl Marx: Selected Writings*, ed. David McLellan (Oxford, UK: Oxford University Press, 2000), 610–16, 615.

168 **In his essay:** Published as 'Theses on the Philosophy of History' (1940), in Walter Benjamin, *Illuminations: Essays and Reflections*, trans. Harry Zohn and ed. Hannah Arendt (New York: Schocken Books, 1969), 253–64.

168 **to the 'angel of history'; 'storm is blowing':** Benjamin, 'Theses on the Philosophy of History', 257, 257–58.

168 **'locomotive of world history':** Quoted in Michael Löwy, *Fire Alarm: Reading Walter Benjamin's 'On the Concept of History'*, trans. Chris Turner (London: Verso Books, 2005), 66–67.

7. HOPE

171 **'Here is Plato's man!':** Diogenes Laertius, *Lives of the Eminent Philosophers*, trans. Pamela Mensch and ed. James Miller (Oxford, UK: Oxford University Press, 2018), 279.

171 **'a waste of time':** Diogenes the Cynic, *Sayings and Anecdotes*, trans. Robin Hard (Oxford, UK: Oxford University Press, 2012), 32.

171 **'citizen of the world':** Diogenes Laertius, *Lives of the Eminent Philosophers*, 288. On the interpretation of this formula, see John L. Moles, 'Cynic Cosmopolitanism', *The Cynics*, ed. R. Bracht Branham and

Marie-Odile Goulet-Cazé (Berkeley, CA: University of California Press, 1996), 105–20.

171 'When asked what is': Diogenes, *Sayings and Anecdotes*, 68.

172 As Hesiod explains: 'The dope': Hesiod, *Works and Days*, trans./ed. A. E. Stallings (London: Penguin, 2018), 21–22, lines 498–501.

172 impossible to place: On the indeterminacy of the myth, even in later retellings, see Dora and Erwin Panofsky, *Pandora's Box: The Changing Aspects of a Mythical Symbol* (Princeton, NJ: Princeton University Press, 1962).

173 a broad consensus: In describing the nature of hope, I have been helped by Luc Bovens, 'The Value of Hope', *Philosophy and Phenomenological Research* 59 (1999): 667–81; Sarah Buss, 'The Irrationality of Unhappiness and the Paradox of Despair', *Journal of Philosophy* 101 (2004): 167–96; Victoria McGeer, 'The Art of Good Hope', *Annals of the American Academy of Political and Social Science* 592 (2004): 100–127; Ariel Meirav, 'The Nature of Hope', *Ratio* 22 (2009): 216–33; and Adrienne M. Martin, *How We Hope: A Moral Psychology* (Princeton, NJ: Princeton University Press, 2013).

173 wholly up to you: A point emphasised in McGeer, 'The Art of Good Hope', 103, and Meirav, 'The Nature of Hope', 228–29.

173 'a passion for what is possible': Søren Kierkegaard, *Fear and Trembling: A Dialectical Lyric* (1843), trans. Robert Payne (University Park, PA: Penn State University Press, 1939), 37.

175 'Hope is not like'; 'hope should shove you': Rebecca Solnit, *Hope in the Dark: Untold Histories, Wild Possibilities* (Chicago: Haymarket Books, 2004; third edition, 2016), 4.

176 'hope and inspiration': Quoted in Solnit, *Hope in the Dark*, xiv.

176 'want you to panic': Greta Thunberg, 'Our House Is On Fire', *No One Is Too Small to Make a Difference* (London: Penguin, 2019), 24.

177 an 'irascible passion': Aquinas, *Summa Theologica*, II-I, q. 40; II-II, qq. 17–22.

177 'at the right times': Aristotle, *Nicomachean Ethics*, trans. David Ross and ed. Lesley Brown (Oxford, UK: Oxford University Press, 2009), 1106b20–23.

178 did not recognise hope: See G. Scott Gravlee, 'Aristotle on Hope', *Journal of the History of Philosophy* 38 (2000): 461–77.

178 Defying the 'angel of history'; 'Angel of Alternate History': Walter Benjamin, 'Theses on the Philosophy of History' (1940), *Illuminations: Essays*

and Reflections, trans. Harry Zohn and ed. Hannah Arendt (New York: Schocken Books, 1969), 253–64, 257; Solnit, *Hope in the Dark*, 71–72.

179 **immortality by 'uploading':** For an excellent account, see Mark O'Connell, *To Be a Machine: Adventures among Cyborgs, Utopians, Hackers, and the Futurists Solving the Modest Problem of Death* (New York: Anchor Books, 2017).

179 **a simple argument:** This argument is based on the 'Branch-Line case' in Derek Parfit's *Reasons and Persons* (Oxford, UK: Oxford University Press, 1984), Part Three, though his own conclusion is more complex.

180 **To paraphrase Franz Kafka:** See Max Brod, *Franz Kafka: A Biography* (Boston: Da Capo Press, 1960), 75: 'Plenty of hope – for God – no end of hope – only not for us'.

180 **'The worst is not':** William Shakespeare, *King Lear* (1606), ed. R. A. Foakes (London: Arden, 1997), 305.

180 **Jonathan Lear calls 'radical hope':** Jonathan Lear, *Radical Hope: Ethics in the Face of Cultural Devastation* (Cambridge, MA: Harvard University Press, 2006), 103.

180 **With Iris Murdoch:** Iris Murdoch, 'Vision and Choice in Morality' (1956), *Existentialists and Mystics: Writings on Philosophy and Literature*, ed. Peter J. Conradi (London: Chatto & Windus, 1997), 76–98, 90.

181 **Life is not a narrative:** Jane Alison, *Meander, Spiral, Explode* (New York: Catapult, 2019), 6.

181 **'I am the one':** Seamus Heaney, *The Cure at Troy: A Version of Sophocles' Philoctetes* (London: Faber and Faber, 1991), 3.

181 **Philoctetes speaks: 'Imagine, son':** Heaney, *The Cure at Troy*, 18.

182 **'Then you're to take':** Heaney, *The Cure at Troy*, 73.

182 **'History says, *Don't hope*':** Heaney, *The Cure at Troy*, 77.

Index

Index

Index